The Writer's Internet

A Creative Guide to the World Wide Web

The Writer's Internet

A Creative Guide to the World Wide Web

Sarah-Beth Watkins

**COMPASS
BOOKS**

Winchester, UK
Washington, USA

First published by Compass Books, 2013
Compass Books is an imprint of John Hunt Publishing Ltd., Laurel House, Station Approach,
Alresford, Hants, SO24 9JH, UK
office1@jhpbooks.net
www.johnhuntpublishing.com
www.compass-books.net

For distributor details and how to order please visit the 'Ordering' section on our website.

Text copyright: Sarah-Beth Watkins 2012

ISBN: 978 1 78099 785 8

A CIP catalogue record for this book is available from the British Library.

Design: Stuart Davies

Printed in the USA by Edwards Brothers Malloy

We operate a distinctive and ethical publishing philosophy in all
areas of our business, from our global network of authors to
production and worldwide distribution.

CONTENTS

Chapter One - The Internet for Writers   1

The History of the Internet   2

What can Writers use it for?   3

Why Bother with the Internet?   7

Who Can Use it?   8

Let's Get Started   9

The Curse of the Constant Browser   10

Moving Forward   11

Chapter Two - Making Money from the Internet   12

Different Types of Writing Jobs

Where to Find Writing Jobs   14

What to Write About   15

What Writing Sells?

The Main Contenders   16

Paying Websites   18

Pay per Post v. Pay per Click   19

Rates of Pay

Bid Sites   20

How You Get Paid   21

It's Not Just About Money

Chapter Three - Writing for the Web   23

Why is the Web different?

Who are your Readers?   24

Crisp, Concise and Clear   25

Writing for the Web

Length and Tone   26

Watch your Grammar   27

British or American spellings? 28

Avoiding Clichés 29

Search Engine Optimisation

Writing for a Response 30

Emoticons and Text Speak

Humour 31

Editing your Work 32

Chapter Four - Fiction on the Net **33**

Writing Stories for Web Viewing

Serialising your Story 34

Novels Online

The Technical Bit 35

Flash Fiction 36

Interactive Fiction 37

Collaborative Fiction

Hypertext Fiction 39

Poetry on the Web

Comments and Feedback 40

Fiction Competitions 41

The Great NaNoWriMo 42

Chapter Five - Research and Information **44**

Why use the Internet for Research?

Using the Internet for Research 45

Double-checking your Facts

Organising your Research 46

Information Gathering by Email 47

Web Directories 48

Article Directories 49

Reference Sites

Specialist Websites 50

Genealogy Sites 51

Online Libraries 52

Archives

Free E-books   53

Doing your Market Research   54

Chapter Six - Education Online   **55**

Courses for Writers

Do you know what kind of Learner you are?   58

Checking Out Your Course   59

Using Online Dictionaries and Thesaurus Sites   60

Translation   61

Checking your Grammar

Just for Fun   62

Finding Writing Guidelines   63

Working as an Online Tutor

Creating your Own Courses   64

Chapter Seven - Forums and Networking   **66**

Why use Social Media for Networking?

The Top Networking Sites   67

The Best Writers' Forums   69

How to Use Them   70

Netiquette   71

Critique Groups   72

Critiquing other Writers' Work   74

Being Careful   75

Chapter Eight - Publishing your E-book   **76**

What is an E-book?

What's the Fuss all About?   77

The Benefits of Publishing your Work as an E-book   79

Preparing your Manuscript   80

Cover Design   82

A Step-by-Step Process

How Much?   83

Where to Sell your E-book 84

Using an E-book Publisher

E-book Rights 86

Chapter Nine - Promoting Yourself Online 87

Using Social Media

Having your own Website 88

Getting Someone Else to Do it! 89

Doing It Yourself 90

Blogging 92

Setting Up Your Own Blog 93

Having your Profile on Other Websites 94

Online Advertising 95

Using Email Newsletters 96

Chapter Ten - Websites, Software and
 Resources for Writers 98

Useful Websites for Writers

Organisations for Writers and Authors 99

Web Directories

Article Directories 100

Reference Sites

Genealogy Sites

Archives 101

Writing Jobs

Free E-books 102

Fiction and Poetry Websites

Humourous Websites 103

Writing Courses 104

Writing Tools and Software

Cloud Services 105

E-book Publishers

E-book Software 106

PDF Converters

Photo Image Sites

Design Software   107

Online Resources for Writers' Block

Dictionary and Thesauri Sites

Website Builders   108

Blogs

Setting up your Own Blog

Profile Websites   109

Grammar Sites

Writing Guidelines

Writers' Forums   110

Critique Sites

The Fun Stuff!

Contacting the Author   111

Dedication

To Jake and Shay for letting me have the computer for more
than five minutes!
And to Stig, without whom this writer would not have the
support to get her manuscript finished.
Love you guys.

Chapter One

The Internet for Writers

The Internet is one of man's greatest inventions. We can now source information, find friends, talk to other writers and look into archives from all around the globe with the click of a mouse. Almost everyone has access to the Internet, whether it is at home, or in a local cafe, hotel or library. It is an amazing tool for writers that is just asking to be used - for sometimes hours on end!

Yet people still have a reluctance to use it to its maximum potential. If you were born in the age before the Internet, it's something that you will have to learn to use rather than having grown up using. Children today use the Internet as easily as turning on the TV. Ok, some TVs actually have the Internet too! But like any new technology, there is a learning process involved but once you begin that process, you are on the way to being Internet savvy.

I took computers as a subject at college in the eighties. Hoorah for word processing, spreadsheets and database! But the Internet? Nowhere to be seen, heard or otherwise used. I have had to keep myself up-to-date with technology and I'm not technically minded. The great thing about the Internet is you learn it from using it and as a writer, I am constantly learning new ways in which it can complement my writing.

And the thing is you don't have to learn everything. A writer doesn't have to be able to build a website from scratch or be able to decode those secret symbols and messages that run on the screen. You can become as skilled as little or as much as you want. All you need to do is to use the Internet for your own purpose, the purpose of being a writer.

This book will show you how by looking at the main ways in which a writer can use the Internet. Whether it's making money or making contacts, the Internet is an increasingly valuable asset to writers and it is not one to be ignored. More and more of our communication occurs across the World Wide Web. Don't get left behind!

The History of the Internet

I'm not going to bore you with a detailed description of the history of the Internet! The early days were complex and technical. If you are interested in a more detailed history, you can look for concise information on Wikipedia or a similar reference site. What I do want to show you is how recent the Internet is.

Hotmail, the first email service, came online in 1996. Google, one of the top search engines, started in 1998. Wikipedia came along in 2001. Then social networking started with the event of MySpace in 2003 followed by Facebook in 2004, although at that time, it was only for college students. YouTube arrived in 2005 and Twitter in 2006. In 2007, the Iphone was launched and mobile web applications began their development.

Today it is estimated that there are over 644 million active websites. The Internet is still a relatively new phenomenon with new sites arriving daily and new developments making it even more accessible and exciting to use. With so much progress in such a short space of time, who knows what the Internet will be capable of in five or ten years time?

I noticed the rapid change in technology more after working as a freelance writer for fifteen years and then taking a break. I had been used to sending out articles and stories by post and including an SAE, waiting anxiously for a positive reply or cheque by return. When I returned to writing, I realised that this wasn't the norm anymore. Magazines wanted email submissions, publishers wanted queries sent in by electronic form and websites just wanted your work! Payment was now electronic or through PayPal and the poor little SAE was a thing of the past. I had to up my Internet skills and start using it to my advantage.

At least I would save on post!

The Internet is something then, that as writers, we can't ignore. It is our newest medium of communication and that includes the written word. As more and more people use the Internet, we need to make sure that we are using it too. It is the medium of the future and a way in which our writing can be brought to a global audience.

What can Writers use it for?

There are many ways in which the Internet can work for you. Here are a few:

- *Making Friends*

  You can find and talk to other writers online, share the ups and downs of producing a masterpiece and support each other in progressing your work. Being connected to other writers can be hugely beneficial in offsetting the times when you are working in solitude.

- *Researching Ideas*

  You have a great idea for a book but its set in ancient Mayan times. What did they wear? Eat? What did their houses look like? Their temples? An Internet search will give you the info you are looking for and you will also be able to see if your idea has already been used by researching books set in the same time period.

- *Earning an Extra Income*

  What writer doesn't want an extra income? There are websites out there that will pay for your contributions in a vast range of subjects and genres. Whether writing blogs, web content, reviews or straight forward articles, there is a market for them.

- *Networking*
  You can make friends but you can also network with other people. The Internet can be used to connect you to other professional people in the book and magazine industries. Communicating with editors and publishers across the Net can only open more doors for you.

- *Creating a Fan-base*
  Social networking can help you to create a fan-base. As writers we all need readers! People who love your writing will want to look you up. Having your own website or blog will attract your readers too.

- *Promoting your Work*
  There are many different ways of promoting your work online like having a website, getting other sites to review your work or having your profile on appropriate pages. Promoting your work online is an opportunity no writer should miss.

- *Promoting Yourself*
  It's not just about your work but about you as a writer. You don't have to have your life story available but posting regular snippets will intrigue and delight your fans. Let people into your world and you create more followers, more readers and ultimately more sales.

- *Healthy Criticism*
  Your work can appear on other websites where readers can leave feedback and comments. Say you have an idea for a fiction novel but you just want to try out the first chapter, you can ask for constructive criticism from other writers and use it to make your writing even better.

- *Learning New Skills*
  There are hundreds of online courses on the Internet that you could take to refresh your skills or to try out a completely new genre.

- *Teaching Others*
  You could also find work tutoring and mentoring other writers. Distance and online colleges often advertise for tutors for their courses. You could even go one step further and create your own.

- *Getting up-to-date news from the World of Writing*
  Signing up to newsletters from publishers, writing sites, job listings, competitions and the like is a way of keeping in touch with what is happening in the wider world of writing. Signing up for newsletters in your particular genre will also keep you well informed.

- *What's On*
  Fancy a trip to a writer's event, conference or workshop? Find out what you can attend in your locality by searching the Web. You might also find local writers' groups or reading circles that you could attend in person when you drag yourself away from the screen!

- *Writers' Retreats and Holidays*
  If you need some peaceful writing time away from it all, you can find writers' retreats and holidays specifically for the genre you write in.

- *Materials and Equipment*
  Shopping had to be mentioned somewhere! There can be some great bargains to be had on the Internet. From ink cartridges to stationary supplies, it's all there.

- *Books and other Reading*
  Books can be purchased too but you can also find free e-books and other documents to download that will aid your research or reading in general.

- *Checking out your Markets*
  Look up magazines, newspapers, script agencies, publishers and TV producers to see what they are looking for and to check style and content of sites that you would like to write for. Access markets across the globe instead of just those in your own country.

- *Accessing Writer's' Guidelines*
  Some publishers of books, magazines and newspapers have guidelines on their websites so that if you are thinking of submitting your work to them, you can see exactly what their requirements are and work towards them.

- *Submitting your Work*
  Many publishers today have electronic submission systems so you can upload your manuscript or proposal to them directly. A great way to save on postage and a much quicker response time to boot.

- *Publishing your own E-book*
  Writers are producing their own work and having it readily available to their readers without going through agents and publishers. Although there are pros and cons to this type of publishing, it's a way of getting your work out there and reaching a global audience. If you decide to publish your own e-book, it will be instantly available to millions of readers across the globe the minute you upload it.

These are just a few ideas and I am sure you will be able to think of other ways in which to use the Internet. There are so many ways in which the Internet complements a writer 's life but are you using it to its full extent?

In later chapters, we will look at all the main areas in which the use of the Internet can aid, support and supplement your writing life. It's there, just waiting to be used, to boost your sales, promote your work and find you new work opportunities. We will look at each of the above areas so that you can benefit your writing life with new ways of working.

Why Bother with the Internet?

Everyone is using the Internet today. You can become familiar with its services and use them to your best ability or you can let the opportunity pass by. There are lots of writers out there that are using it to their advantage and you can be one of them.

It doesn't have to be the only way in which you write and have your work available to the general public but when you're a writer, doesn't every opportunity to have your work read count?

The Internet opens up a new world of opportunity - a global world of opportunity. You can make contacts with writers in Italy, Africa and India or send your work to markets in America, Canada and Ireland. Pick a country, any country, and the World Wide Web can take you there.

This can work for you in many ways. For example, an Italian writer friend of mine was recently working on a book that had Native American characters.

My story is set in the Prohibition Era, Chicago, and there would have been no chance to write it based on the material available in Italy, which amounts to nothing. But with the Internet I could research the subjects online, I could browse through databases and lists of books, including novels of the time. I could buy these books from international bookstores and even look through the material from a few institutions - like the American Library of Congress - only online.(Sarah Zama - writer)

She used the Internet to research Native American history but was still uncertain of whether her characters were coming across as authentic. Through a critique website, she found a Native American lady who not only helped her with her research but read through her manuscript to make sure the characters were as real and genuine as they could be. This couldn't have happened without the Internet. The connections you make can aid your writing, support you as a writer and take your work to readers wherever they may live.

Who Can Use It?

It might be too general to say everyone again but it is accessible to the majority of people in the world in some shape or form. I was lucky enough to be asked to join a delegation of women who were travelling to Tanzania to investigate women's development in Third World countries. As well as giving presentations, my job was to write up the visit for various magazines and websites to publicise the issues women were facing. I was amazed to arrive in remote villages in Africa where there were Internet shacks or a satellite dish adorning a mud hut. It might not have been the best connection in the world but it worked.

As well as being widely available, the technology of computers also makes it easier for people to use that might otherwise be put off. If you hate typing or have arthritis in your hands, you can use voice recognition software that types for you. Eyes not as great as they were? Then larger fonts can be used and keyboards with larger than average keys.

Personally, I began using the Internet far more after I had surgery and was going through a long recovery period. I couldn't attend meetings, writer 's' groups or tutor classes as I had done previously. The Internet became a lifeline. I could chat to other writers, email them some of my writing for criticism, provide articles for various websites, write reviews, submit my work online and tutor distance learning courses. A bigger, broader world of writing opened up to me and I haven't looked back since.

Let's Get Started

So hopefully you have a computer with Internet capability, whether in the form of a landline connection, satellite or mobile service, or you have access to such. Your location will determine the best way you can access the Internet but look around for the best packages in terms of cost and connectivity.

I used a mobile connection for years until I found that the articles I was writing for a particular website needed photos attached to them. I would sit for hours trying to get a picture alongside my writing until I realised - duh! - I had a mobile connection. Off I drove with my laptop and mobile modem until I hit on the best connection. It just so happened to be down at my local beach. So every morning, I wrote my articles and then sat watching the waves whilst photos uploaded. It might sound idyllic to have such a view whilst working but as soon as satellite broadband was available in my area, I signed up!

Once you have a good connection, you will use a search engine to retrieve information on the Internet. Search engines like Google, Yahoo, AOL, Ask, Bing and Altavista crawl the web looking for sites and links to add to their index. When you type in a search term, for instance, 'writing website', the search engine looks through its indexes for a match and then displays all that it has found for you in a list of the most relevant matches.

The results you get differ depending on the search engine you are using. To find the one that suits you best or seems to turn up the most relevant results, you need to experiment with using a few different ones.

Once you have settled on the search engine that is appropriate for you, you need to set it as your home page so that every time you open your web browser, it's there just waiting for you to ask it to work for you. Some search engines have a 'set us as your homepage' button to click on whilst others you will have to tell your browser to use.

Decide on the best search engine for your browsing and practice with writer relevant searches. We will look at specific websites and different types of websites for writers throughout this book but get started by searching with keywords such as 'writer ', 'writing' and 'writing opportunities' to see what you can find.

The Curse of the Constant Browser

Who hasn't spent hours looking for one thing on the Internet and find that they have gone on to look at a hundred more? That may be excessive but with information at the click of a button, it is so easy to browse and browse and browse...

So a word of warning here. Know what you are looking for before you start searching. Have a list of your key words or questions, sites you want to find or info that you are looking for. You will inevitably find yourself going off at a tangent at some point but as long as you get what you initially turned the computer on for in the first place then you have achieved your purpose.

If you are using your computer during a day where you also have a deadline looming, an idea that needs fleshing out or a serious writing session ahead then set a time limit. Give yourself an hour, two at the maximum, to devote to the Internet but once your time is up, stop browsing! The Internet can eat into your precious writing time but only if you let it. Remember the computer is a machine and you are the boss (for the time being, anyway!).

Moving Forward

This book has been written so that you can read it as a whole or dip into the chapters that are most relevant to you. Throughout the chapters, web sites will be mentioned with their addresses but these are compiled again in the final chapter for quick reference. I have looked up the best web sites for writers and the ones that are the easiest to use. Some you will love and some maybe not so much but as you use the Internet more, you will find which sites work best for you and which ones you will get the most out of.

I've tried not to be too technical in any of our discussions about the Internet as this book is primarily for writers who are not computer geniuses and just want to get the most of its use. Remember that the use of any new technology will be a learning curve but I'll be on that curve with you, helping you out with tips and advice on the way. Welcome to the Writer's Internet!

Chapter Two

Making Money from the Internet

How would you like to make money writing for the World Wide Web? It won't make you a millionaire but there is a chance of earning an extra, regular income from your writing. Web sites and content providers need writers. The opportunities are out there. To make money from the Net, you have to look for those opportunities and weigh up their worth. Time is money. Have you got writing time to spare?

Different Types of Writing Jobs

There are several different types of writing jobs that will appear on the World Wide Web. Here are a few of the most common opportunities that you will find:

- *Writing Articles* - the majority of writing jobs on the Net are for informative, fact based articles. There are also jobs for article re-writers who take an article and revamp it into a new original piece of work.
- *Reviewing* - reviews of products, hotels, travel companies, plays, movies and books are in demand across the Web. Some are fact-based; others ask for your personal opinion and often include rating systems.
- *Stories* - fiction is growing on the Net and there are many web sites now dedicated to showcasing new writers' work. For fiction writers, this can be a great way to create a fan-base before looking at publishing their novels.
- *Web Content* - web sites need words. Web site owners need content that attract readers and encourages them to use their services. If you are web literate, you can find work writing the content for other people's web sites.

- *Blogs* - a blog is a journal or diary type of regular entry that is usually updated daily. They can be on a particular subject giving out information or can include more personal opinion pieces. Many writers have their own blogs to promote themselves and their writing but there is also work out there for writers who can commit to keeping an up-to-date blog on a particular subject and supplement it with photos, images or videos as well.

- *Social Media* - you can actually get writing jobs using social media. Some companies and individuals are too busy to write their own tweets or regularly update their Facebook pages. You might have to pretend to be someone else but hey, isn't writing all about creativity?

- *Academic Essays* - an area of great debate. There are some online companies that pay writers to compile school and university essays. These services are used by students who get a well written essay for their money. However, colleges and universities have strict rules about plagiarism and whilst the students haven't exactly copied your work, they are passing it off as their own.

- *Online Tutoring* - ok, so this isn't exactly writing, more like correcting but if you can get the work, it's a great way of passing on your skills and helping others in the process. Various colleges and universities run online courses and some companies directly sell adult distance learning courses through the medium of the Internet. They may use certain types of software for corrections or utilise interactive forums to facilitate conversations between their tutors and students. To apply for this type of job, you will need a certain level of computer savvy as well as expertise in a specific subject area.

- *Allsorts* - you can find writing jobs on the Net that cover all aspects of writing like CV writing, speech writing, business presentations, technical writing, the preparation of technical manuals, etc. You might find the job online but it could be for work that is done offline. Search and ye shall find!

Where to Find Writing Jobs

You can always search the Internet for writing jobs and your search results may turn up some gems or the same old ads. Regular job web sites may also turn up possibilities by using the terms 'writer ', 'editor ' or 'author '. A better way to find writing jobs is to bookmark pages that are written by writers or especially target writers with regularly updated job spots.

Freelancewritinggigs.com is a web site that posts online jobs for writers on a daily basis. At a recent glance, jobs included an acupuncture content writer, article re-writers, an education blogger, a celebrity diet and workout writer, freelance business writers, a copywriter for a non-profit business start-up, a short stories' editor, a proof-reader, reporters and technical writers. Something for everyone!

Freelancewriting.com also has a range of jobs that are posted daily. The search can be narrowed down by looking at their lists of freelance, online and blogging jobs. I've also used This site has the usual lists of freelance, article and blogging jobs available but it also has lists for travel writers, authors, ghost writers, proof-reading, PR and other types of writing opportunities.

Another type of web site that offers writing jobs is Craig's List, a community classifieds site. Craigslist is a worldwide network of ads in all different categories that are posted daily. Type in 'Craig's List' in your search bar and the most relevant one for your area should turn up at the top of your search results. In America especially, more and more editors and publishers are using this web site to advertise not only located jobs but online work as well. There are some doozies here but there are also some gems. Sort through the lists to find jobs worth applying for.

Writers also post lists of companies up on the Internet that they have worked for or researched to find out what writing opportunities they offer. Browse sites of actual web writers to see who and what they recommend.

What to Write About

Well, anything goes! The Internet really is a place where any type of writing does and can exist. It isn't regulated and that can lead to web pages of the extreme kind being written and posted on the World Wide Web. While there is a negative side to web writing, there is a much more positive one in that you have carte blanche to write about your interests, hobbies, skills and other areas of expertise.

When you sign up for a web writing job, you are likely to be asked what your subject areas are and will be presented with a list from which you can choose areas you wish to write about. You can write on subjects you are very familiar with or take time out to research new subjects and build up your expertise in a new area.

I have written articles on arts & crafts, education, health, writing, relationships, birthday parties, weddings, gardening, wine-making - even the best types of petrol-driven remote control cars! The list goes on. It's amazing how much knowledge you amass over the years that can be turned into short, informative web articles.

So you get to choose. Start by writing a list of what you feel most comfortable writing about. Think about subjects that you have a general knowledge of and then break each subject heading down into specific topics. When you sign up with a web writing company, you'll have a ready list of subjects you can get to work on straightaway.

What Writing Sells?

In the next chapter, we will look at how to write for the Internet with regard to style, length and other factors. If you are already a writer, working away on articles or stories for print, you already have the skills to write for the Internet. A good command of language, grammar and syntax, a way with words and a natural ability to come up with new ideas are all essential to being a good writer. It is no different with web writing.

Your writing needs to be clear and concise, to the point and it must encapsulate information in so few words. Web writing, by its nature, is far shorter than article writing. Articles can be as little as 200 words, with 250 - 500 being the average word count. You will also find that you need to work to a strict deadline and will be required to produce work on a regular basis. But if you can do this, you can write for the Internet and the writing that sells will be yours.

I began my web writing career in the early days when the Internet was a new invention and web sites were crying out for writers. I was already working for a magazine that decided to run its own web site. I was asked to contribute shorter pieces than I was used to, going down from 1,200 words to 300 words. And I was paid a ridiculous amount of money for each piece. It was great!

But it didn't last. The company changed hands and the web writing opportunities dried up. One of the issues with writing for web sites is that they come and go. You're just getting used to writing for one when they go belly up and you have to search for new writing avenues but there are plenty out there. It's just a matter of chasing them down.

The Main Contenders

If you ask a web writer who comes to mind when they think of writing for the Internet, some top names will come up. These are companies that regularly take on writers for their own web sites or they provide content to other clients.

- *Demand Media Studios* (www.demandstudios.com) - uses writers, filmmakers, bloggers and copy-editors to provide content for other web sites.
- *About* (www.about.com) - an information site that has two levels of writers; guides and topic writers plus video directors.
- *Words of Worth* (www.wordsofworth.co.uk) - is a content delivery company offering work to freelance writers from around the world.
- *Squidoo* (www.squidoo.com) - helps writers to create their own web pages, each one about a subject or story or opinion that they know and love. When one of the pages does well, it earns a royalty for the writer or for a charity
- *Hubpages* (www.hubpages.com) - 'hubbers' produce their own pages to receive revenue and recognition through a HubScore ranking system.
- *Textbroker* (www.textbroker.com) - an article writing service that offers writers a four tiered payment structure and opportunities for proofreading jobs.
- *Constant Content* (www.constant-content.com) - writers can add to a catalogue of SEO friendly articles that are available for sale to web publishers and make money on their own articles.

Some of these companies use your articles for their own pages, some sell your work onto other clients and others help you to create your own web pages that then generate a revenue payment. Registration is usually free although you will have to provide a writing sample and/ or CV. You then have an author 's area that you will access to choose writing projects or upload your own work. The amount of help you are given varies but every site should have some sort of writers' guidelines.

I used to provide content for one company who posted article titles every morning. You could select which articles you would like to write and were given three days to complete them in. You could write directly into an electronic submissions template and a list of keywords that had to be included in the body of the article was given. All you had to do then was come up with 250 words of text - simples!

Of course, there are many other web sites and content providers out there and their methods vary but the above companies are a few that regularly take on new writers, provide online supports and have been known to give you access to regular work. Check out which countries they take writers from. Some are specifically looking for US and Canadian writers, others are looking for UK writers and yet others will employ writers from around the globe.

Paying Web Sites

The main contenders listed above are web sites that recruit writers to provide content for their sites and those of their clients but some web sites do directly pay for your articles and stories in the same way as they would if you were submitting to a magazine or newspaper.

To find web sites that cover your subject area, conduct a general search then once you are into their site, look for writers' guidelines or writer submissions. If you can't see any sign of them taking freelance writers, send a quick email to the editor with your ideas. If they are interested, they will get back to you.

On a recent search, I found web sites such as www.wisegeek.com, all looking for writers. Families.com wants bloggers to write 300 word articles to cover over 30 topics including parenting, family fun, marriage and home and garden. They pay per blog entry and have a training period for new writers.

Wisegeek.com is one of those web sites that just has thousands of articles on many different subjects including business, languages, crafts, health, beauty, sports and hobbies. Full guidelines on writing for them and information on the application process can be found at www.wisegeek.com/freelance-writingjobs.htm.

Writing-world.com is different in that it takes full length articles on all aspects of the writing business for their email newsletter. They also pay per article but ask that you write between 800 - 2,000 words. Check out their detailed contributor's guidelines if you have ideas for in-depth articles that other writers would like to read.

Pay per Post v. Pay per Click

There are two main ways of making an income by writing articles for the Internet. One is more immediate, the other long-term. Getting paid per post means you are paid a set price for a set project. So you agree to write a 300 word article and know you are going to be paid $15 for writing it. That's money in the bank, usually paid on a monthly basis, when all your article sales are added up and your total is deposited into your account.

Pay per click is also known as revenue share and for this kind of article, there is no immediate payment. You earn from people clicking onto your page and reading your article. Payment per click is very low but your earnings accumulate over the long-term. It is a continual process where your work continues to earn payment as long as it is being viewed.

There is a tendency for new web writers to go for jobs that are pay per post but more and more writers, as they become more computer savvy, are trying out pay per click. The trick is to get people to read your page and that involves use of social networking. Once you start using social sites like Facebook and Twitter, you'll soon pick up new skills and become addicted! More about social networking in chapter seven.

Rates of Pay

This is a tricky one because every web site or content provider is different. Some as we have seen are revenue share, some are pay per post. Some operate a tiered paying system whilst others pay a flat fee for a set piece of work. Payment can be per article or per word per article and therefore paid according to length.

Always check the rates of pay before applying for an Internet writing job. There are good payers and there are bad. I once wrote for a company that only paid $5 a post but the thing was they only wanted articles of 250 words on subjects I was completely familiar with. I could write three or four articles a day in less than an hour making an average earning of $100 a week. Not bad for a small job.

You really need to weigh up your time versus your payment. If it's going to take you three hours to write an article you're going to get paid $15 - is it worth it? However, if that article can be done in 15 minutes and you can write 20 a day, that's a daily income of $280. Short pieces of writing may look like they are poorly paid but if you can write consistently and maintain a high out-put, you can generate a sizeable income.

Just don't sell yourself short. Many ads for writers ask for free contributions or are only paying a few cents. This can be great if you are building a portfolio or trying your skills out on a new subject or area but in the long run, it will do you no favours. Writing is like any other profession, it has its standards and its minimum charges.

Bid Sites

I don't like them but I know people who have used their services and apply for the jobs on them that are happy with their use. Bid sites are sites where people advertise jobs they have. It could be CV writing, help with a novel, scriptwriting, technical writing or many other different jobs. The jobs are often in bulk so you might be asked to contribute 50 articles over the course of a month for a set fee. The clients post how many articles they want, what subjects they want written about, their budget and the timescale and you cost it accordingly and send your bid in. They then select the bidder who gives them the most value for money.

The idea is that you place a bid for the work alongside other potential writers.

The problem with these sites is that the bids go in at a very low rate. No-one in their right mind wants to be paid $5 for a 10,000 word article but that's what people bid. The work is extremely low paid and I don't know of anyone who has made a decent income from writing for these kinds of web sites.

However, they are worth looking at as registration is usually free and it doesn't cost you to browse for writing opportunities. I have known writers who started by bidding for work, built up regular contributions with a specific company and then negotiated further work privately, away from the conventions of the bidding site and at a rate that suited them.

How You Get Paid

PayPal is used by the majority of content providers and web site companies. Although some do still pay by cheque, PayPal has become the most secure and efficient way of paying writers who are situated around the globe. It is easy to open an account and all transactions occur online. All account details are secure with PayPal and they are never disclosed to a third party, giving your account maximum protection.

When you work for web companies, you may get paid in dollars, euros, pounds or the currency of whatever country their head office operates in. Whatever currency you are paid in, you can leave in your PayPal account for online shopping or have it deposited into your regular bank account. The currency will be converted into your own and you'll be ready to spend!

It's Not Just About Money

Oh, yes it is, I hear you cry! But hang on a minute, there is the portfolio aspect to consider. Quite often when you apply for the top online writing jobs or you want to join a content writing programme, they'll want to see your CV and proof that you have written for other web sites. If you have a list of links that can direct an editor to your previous work, it shows that you are a published web writer and it might just make or break your application. The more you write for the Internet, the more work you can apply for with proof of previous successes.

There are also writing jobs that might not pay but have extra benefits. I review four books a month for an American mind, body and spirit web site. I don't get paid but I do get a regular supply of new, hot-off-the-press books to read and review. I receive around $80 worth of books a month for free! For an avid reader like me, who buys books like other women buy shoes; this is a fantastic way of writing for the web and saving on my inevitable Amazon bill.

It never hurts to write some freebies even if your ultimate aim is to make a few bucks!

Chapter Three

Writing for the Web

Writing for the Web differs from writing for print because people read web pages differently. The Internet is more immediate, quicker to use and readers who use it are looking for information that they can read in an instant. They scan sites to find what they want and read them just as quickly. If your writing does not appeal to someone browsing the Internet in the first few seconds of their search, they'll click onto something else. Knowing how to write for the Web will boost your chances of sales and make sure your readers stay on your page.

Why is the Web different?

We have mentioned that using the Internet as a resource for reading is a much more immediate experience than reading a book but the way we physically use the Internet also makes a difference. We don't read web pages the same way in which we read a book. Computer screens sit at a distance further away from our eyes. The shape is different too; a computer screen is landscape size rather than the portrait style that we are used to reading in books and newspapers.

When we use the Internet, we scan pages for the information that we want rather than reading the whole text. We generally look down the left hand side of a page to pick out any of the key words we are looking for and then look horizontally to find more information on the subject we are browsing. Although scanning is quicker than reading, the process of actually reading on a computer screen is said to be up to 25 per cent slower than if you were reading a book. And we live in an impatient world. We expect the Internet to deliver up answers quickly and if it doesn't, we click elsewhere. We don't click on a web site expecting to still be on it half an hour later reading its most informative article. We'll read a bit of that then click to another page or site and fill ourselves up with bite sized pieces of information.

Screens are also visually fuzzier than printed material so much consideration is given to font and size to make reading an easy experience. Website designers spend hours making sites look attractive with the use of photos and images. Sound and background music may also play a part in making text look more attractive.

A page needs to be visually appealing in order for a reader to stick with the information it is portraying. The writing not only has to read well but look good. You won't have to worry about the visuals if you are writing for a content company - their website will be up and running for you to add to - but if you are creating your own website, it's something to consider. We'll look more at having your own website in chapter nine.

Who are your Readers?

When you are writing web articles, you need to bear in mind who will be reading them. It's the same as doing your market research when writing for magazines. Who is the website aimed at? What kind of information will they be looking for? What kind of tone and style will appeal to them?

A website for teenagers is going to be vastly different from a website for new mums. Likewise, a website aimed at doctors is going to be different to one that is used by people interested in alternative medicine. Know the website that you are writing for and write for their readership.

One way of finding out more about website readers is to look at any forums or comments that they have contributed to. From these, you will get a feel of what is important to their website users and what information they might be looking for or what subjects they want to know more about.

Are there ads on the page? These also give you information on what the readers of any particular web page are looking for. Knowing who your readers are will help you to develop writing that speaks specifically to them.

Crisp, Concise and Clear

Web writing needs to be as clear and concise as you can make it. You will never know the literacy level of your reader, whether English is their second language or whether their culture is far removed from yours, which is why your writing must be understandable and to the point.

Even if you are writing about business, finance or technical issues, that stray into jargon using territory, you can keep your text crisp and clear. The subject matter you are writing about might be complex but the way in which you write it can still illuminate the subject for the most novice reader.

Use unambiguous words in short and simple sentences. Use strong verbs instead of weak ones and be as precise as you can. Make sure every word is there for a reason and cut out those that aren't essential to the text.

Your job is to make the reading experience as simple and easy as possible. Readers who come across words they don't know or big blocks of text that will strain their eyes to read, will automatically click onto another page. If you are earning through a revenue process, this is the last thing you want. You want readers to enjoy your articles and click onto more articles that you have written. If you give them what they want then you will have more success as a Web writer.

Writing for the Web

There are style guidelines to use when writing for the Web. Writing for the Internet isn't as complicated as it may seem and it will become second nature to you once you get started. All the conventions below will just become part of your knowledge and will build up your Web writing skills. Here are some key points to remember:

- The most important information goes at the top of a web article
- The first sentence should answer any question that has been asked
- Short, compact paragraphs are essential
- Sentences should be simple and concise
- Subheadings are used to regularly break up paragraphs - more than they would appear in a printed article
- Use Arial or Times New Roman fonts unless otherwise indicated
- Don't use italics, change fonts, colour words or make any other changes to your text that make it look fussy and unreadable
- Use Plain English, no jargon
- Use short words instead of long-winded ones
- Cut out all extraneous words
- Don't underline - that's for links
- Links to websites can be included (and underlined!)
- Don't use block capitals - it's like shouting
- Key words can be used so a search engine can index the article
- Be absolutely clear and concise, utilising every word to maximum effect

Length and Tone

Everything is shorter on the Internet. Articles are generally 250 - 350 words. (As I write this I've just been asked to write an article of 500 words for Facebook so ok, longer articles exist.) This means condensing factual information into bite-sized pieces. Longer articles are sometimes used but people do not tend to stay on a website long enough to read full length articles or stories. Longer pieces of writing, when offered, are usually downloadable as a

PDF or similar file. They are then looked at offline or printed off to be read when sitting in a more comfortable position.

The tone of web articles are much more friendly and conversational than printed articles. There is a greater use of the first person 'I' and the first person plural 'We'. The second person 'You' is also used especially in how-to and instructional articles. This is so that when we read web articles, they sound like someone is talking to us. We might not know who but we expect to find information that is presented as if talking to us like an equal.

Every site that you write for will also have its own style. I wrote how-to articles for awhile and they were quite directive. You do this...then you do that...step by step instructions on how to. When I started reviewing, I took that tone with me and was told that it sounded too much like I was giving out orders! A quick rethink of my style and pointers from a great editor got me on the right track.

Look at the other articles that have been written for the web site that you want to work for and you will see the kind of tone and style that their readers like. Checking your market before you submit any work will ensure that your writing is appropriate for them.

Watch your Grammar

Don't close the book because I've said the 'G' word! How many of us, even as writers, hate the thought of grammar? English lessons tortured pupils into correct grammar usage and it's like any subject that becomes painful, we shy away from having anything to do with it.

But of course, all writers have a duty to use good grammar. There has been a sense that Web writing doesn't have to be as correct as writing for books or magazines but why shouldn't it? It is still a written medium and as writers for that medium, we should be setting good standards and making sure that our own writing is as perfect as it can be.

One common grammatical mistake that many Web writers make is writing in a passive voice instead of the active.

Passive - The boat was repaired by Martin & Sons.

Active - Martin & Sons repaired the boat.

Passive - Italy has been visited by tourists on many occasions.

Active - Tourists have visited Italy on many occasions.

Active sentences put the person or persons doing the action first rather than the subject. Their focus is on the 'who' instead of the 'what'. It makes your writing more immediate and cuts down on the clutter of extraneous words.

If you need to practice your grammar, have a look at my suggested sites in chapter six. Reading books like *Eats, Shoots & Leaves* by Lynne Truss will also help you to brush up on your skills.

British or American spellings?

I use British spellings as a rule but then I am based in Ireland. The thing with the Internet, of course, is that it is global. You might find a website that you want to write for but they are American and so you will have to adapt your writing to suit and vice versa.

Whatever spellings you are using, be consistent and get yourself a copy of a good British/ American language guide. When I started writing reviews for an American website, I was asked to use US spellings. You can set Microsoft Word to spell-check in various languages so I set mine to American for some extra help. However, I didn't realise the variation in punctuation and grammar rules. I was lucky enough to have an editor that would regularly point out what I was doing wrong and the experience has meant I can now write in either language.

When you are researching who to write for or applying for a Web writer position, be aware of which language they prefer and make sure you use it correctly. If you can use both British and American spellings, you are opening up your work to even more potential markets and a greater chance of employment.

Avoiding Clichés

I have to admit, I use them. I like clichés but they have been done to death (!). They are just so common in our speech that we use them too readily when we begin to write. We even use them without realising it.

Clichés are phrases or expressions that have been so over-used that they have lost their original meaning. For instance, when actors say 'break a leg' or when times are tough and you comment 'it never rains but it pours'. These are sayings that have no real meaning anymore and their use in Web writing muddies waters that should be clear!

Check over your writing for clichés and if it can be said in a more original, unique way then delete them and add in an alternative. Writing for the Internet is about writing clear and concise copy. No extra words, and unfortunately, clichés are extra words that should be avoided.

Search Engine Optimisation (SEO)

Search Engine Optimisation is a process that makes websites more visible to search engines. Wait, I'm not going to get complicated on you! What writers need to know about this is that search engines crawl the Web looking for things to index and they look for keywords. So they find a site and go yeah, this must be about parenting...or whatever it is because they are picking up on the most appropriate words.

You might be asked to add keywords into your articles or reviews. Hopefully, you will just be given a list and then it's just a matter of inserting them within your text while ensuring that it is still readable. But you may also be asked to write SEO ready pieces or you might find that whilst looking for jobs online, these are some of the most available positions.

The trick with writing SEO copy is to think about what words a person would use to look up an article. Say you wanted to find an article on the best secondary schools in the London area. Your keywords are 'secondary', 'school' and 'London'. You could also add in related terms like 'education', 'second level', 'teaching', and then more specific subjects or areas. Think about what words a person would ask a search engine to look for in order to come up with a list of options. A writer that can provide articles that are SEO friendly stands a better chance of having their work used.

Writing for a Response

Some articles, copy or reviews are written to provoke a response from the reader. I don't mean that you shut your computer down in a rage or swear you will never use the Internet again!

Their purpose might be to click on a link to purchase a product or to download a document. It could be that it is written as sort of an advert to then divert readers through to another website. This type of writing requires that there is a prompt to action. Even a short piece about arts & crafts will be written to spur on the reader to try it out for themselves.

If the company you're working for wants readers to sign up for a newsletter or fill out a questionnaire, they will tell you to include directions on how to do so in your copy. Including links can be just a matter of you typing in a website address into your article. The website owners will do the actual work of making sure the link works.

Emoticons and Text Speak

No, no and no! I've just had a Facebook conversation with a friend using text speak. One, because it's quicker and two, because I'm trying to get rid of them so I can type this! You can use emoticons and text speak in your own personal conversations but never, ever in Web articles. I wouldn't even use it to Tweet or talk to colleagues. It doesn't look professional, makes you seem like you're 16 and as I think everyone knows - I'm way, way past that milestone!

As we've discussed, web writing is about clear and concise copy and text speak just isn't good practice. Words are incorrectly spelt, shortened and abbreviated and not everyone knows what they mean. I spent hours last night trying to work out what YOLO stood for. My son received it in a message and since he thinks I'm good with words, I was supposed to know the answer. I started trying things like *you old lazy oddbod, you only love Oreos, yachts or landrovers ok* but nothing made sense. It wasn't until another friend told him it means *you only live once* that we understood what the message said. It's like using jargon, if there's any chance that your readers won't understand what you are writing about, then leave well alone.

Humour

I love reading articles that have a sense of humour to them. I wrote parenting articles for a while that gave other parents a laugh but humour just doesn't seem to be the done thing anymore. Editors are wary of humourous articles. The problem with humour is that everyone has their own sense of it and it may not be the next person's. So as not to put off prospective readers, web articles tend to be more straightforward with the funnies left out.

However, if you like humour writing and think you can give it a shot; there are two great websites that are open to contributions. The first is an American site, full of articles, videos and photo-shopped graphics. It covers categories such as history, sport, celebs, music and science plus others. Writers are welcomed in all genres so there's something for everyone here.

The other is a spoof news website, which makes you laugh out loud. They provide writers' guide- lines and have a writer 's room where you can post your news funnies onto a submissions board. The most voted for article gets the accolade of Writer of the Month.

There are other humourous websites out there if you search for them. Check out any writers' guidelines they may have or details on how to submit your work if you would like to try out this genre. Everyone needs a laugh at times!

Editing your Work

As with any type of writing, once you have finished your master-piece, you need to go through an editing process. Even though web articles are shorter than your average magazine article, they still need due care and attention. The issue with editing web articles is that you might not have much time between accepting a piece of work and getting your article into an editor. One of the sites I have written for gives you 2 - 3 days but I know others that just give you a day.

However little time you have, you can still edit. Write your piece and then leave it to one side, even if it's just to grab a coffee or take the dog for a quick walk. When you come back to it with fresh eyes, you will see more clearly any changes that need to be made. Try to do this two or three times before you send it in.

Copyscape is a free plagiarism checker that can also help you out with the editing process. It can be downloaded from It searches for existing content online to make sure that your article is original and authentic. Editors use it to ensure that articles have not been posted online before but you can also use it to check the originality of the content you are providing. With a little extra work, you can make sure that what you are writing really is something new that will attract your readers.

Chapter Four

Fiction on the Net

Fiction on the Net has taken off surprisingly well since most people don't have the time to read through long passages on a computer screen nor do they find it comfortable to do so. Fiction has adapted and developed into other forms especially for World Wide Web users. The Internet has opened up new ways for writers to express themselves and showcase their work from interactive fiction to shape-shifting poetry.

Writing Stories for Web Viewing

Stories for the Web are no different to the stories you would write for a magazine. Let me clarify that. Yes, there are differences in length and presentation and some of the new formats are more innovative and interactive but a story written for whatever format is still a story.

It needs characters, good description, an interesting setting, believable dialogue, plot, structure, a clear point of view and a great opening paragraph or hook to draw your readers in.

Stories appearing on the Internet need to be well written and attention grabbing so that readers stay on that particular website, whether it is yours or one you have posted your work on. Your writing needs to be as good as you can make it. Remember that your title is the first thing that a reader will see of your story. It's going to be listed under its genre or a list of new stories posted so it makes sense to really work on your title and make sure that it sticks out from the crowd. Spend time on making it intriguing and exciting so that a web page user thinks 'I'll click right here' because it sounds like a good read.

Readability is important. As we have seen with articles that are written for the web, paragraphs need to be short and sweet.

The text needs to be broken up regularly with spacing, making your story easier on the eye. While you may not be directly responsible for the layout of your story, you will need to write it bearing in mind that it needs to have shorter sentences and paragraphs than in print. In a story of a low word count, every word counts! Your story should read well but flow smoothly.

Browse Fiction on the Web (www.fictionontheweb.co.uk) for examples of well constructed stories written especially for the Internet. They post a new story every Tuesday, Friday and Sunday for your perusal. They are always open to new submissions but the genres they are looking for do change so check out their submissions section for up-to-date information.

Serialising your Story

Many writers have found that serialising their story connects them to more readers and a growing fan-base. You can serialise your story by using your own website, a blog, Facebook or other social media. The idea is to regularly post your story section by section until the full manuscript is available to read online.

Posts are short, 500 - 1,000 words long, and are written with great openings and end on a cliff-hanger. Each ending makes the reader who found your page want to log on again to read the next part and the next...

You won't make any money from your story this way but you will build up an audience who can comment and give you feedback on your work. Once your story is fully developed you can then look for a publisher and use your posts as part of your biography and achievements.

Novels Online

If you want to write a novel that will be available online, you are really looking at producing an e-book. Unless you are serialising a story that ends up at novel length, readers just won't want to sit in front of the computer staring at a screen for hours to get to the end of your work.

In chapter eight, we will look at publishing your own e-book. These can then be downloaded to a Kindle, Sony E-reader or other electronic reading device or they can be downloaded and printed off to be read at a later date. Given that it's not cost effective or eco-friendly to be printing off reams of paper, the majority of your readers will be using e-book devices. If you are hoping to get into this market, get a reader or ask a friend to show you theirs and start looking at how other writers have produced their work for this format.

There is great debate amongst writers about printed books versus e-books. Some people think that e-books are the books of the future and that they spell the demise of the printed book. Others hold on to their love of the printed word and vow that this will never happen. Even though I read e-books and use the Internet as a freelance writer, I have to say I still love printed books for reading in bed, in the bath, and out on a sun lounger. Using an e-reader just doesn't feel as cosy and relaxing. What side of the debate are you on?

The Technical Bit

In order to send your stories to a web editor, you are either going to have to attach them as an email or paste them into the body of an email text. Editors can be very fussy about how you approach them so always look at their submission guidelines. Some companies don't like to open emails because of the risk of a virus attacking their computers but others will - presumably those with good antivirus software.

Files usually opened by web editors are .doc, .rtf or rich text. Some will also work with .docx files but not all. To be on the safe side, I send all my work in as doc files. Check out any website guidelines and submission details to find out the correct file type for your story. If an editor won't directly take a Word document, you can easily change it to their required file type. When you click on 'save as' in Word, it will give you a list of different file types to choose from and you can select the editor 's preference from there.

Stories should still be as well presented as if you were sending in a paper submission. A typical font like Times New Roman, Tahoma or Arial are fine in 12 point, double spaced and left aligned. Again, different editors want different things so always read any guidelines or submission details before you hit the enter key.

Flash Fiction

Flash fiction are short, bite sized stories that people can read quickly. In general, these stories range from 300 - 1,000 words and can be found in many genres and forms. Writing a story in so few words is an art in itself. There's no time to build up characters and have lengthy descriptions but still a story can be told in its entirety.

Flash Fiction Online (www.flashfictiononline.com) is a website that showcases new writers (and old) whose stories range from 500 - 1,000 words long. This website aims to promote flash fiction and short stories that contain the key elements of characters, plot and setting. Look through their back issues and current stories for a feel of how to write these short, short stories.

Flash Fiction (www.flashfiction.net) states on its website that it has a singular mission: *to prepare writers, readers, editors, and fans for the imminent rise to power of that machine of compression, that hugest of things in the tiniest of spaces: flash freakin' fiction!* There are some great stories on this site and they only take a few minutes to read.

If you're ready to write your own flash fiction and get it posted online, Backhand Stories (www.backhandstories.com) are open to submissions but they say they should be thought-provoking, innovate and yes, you guessed it, short! Check out their web site for submission details.

There are even stories as short as a few words - the size of a Tweet. One author, who I regularly read, is Arjun Basu (@arjunbasu), who sends out the shortest of short stories through Twitter. These fiction bites are known as twisters and are never more than 140 characters long. If like me, you enjoy short bursts of fiction, then follow Arjun on Twitter for some award-winning short stories. You can even start story tweeting yourself!

Interactive Fiction

Interactive fiction is the name more commonly given to stories that play out like role-playing games. Rather than just text, they can be graphical and urge the user to click on elements within the graphics or text to continue the story. For instance, you may have to knock on a door, open a letter or converse with a character. You play the main character in the story and make choices as to where the story goes.

This type of fiction is available in lots of genres from fantasy to thrillers and varying styles from the light-hearted to the serious. Some popular games are Galatea, Photopia, Slouching towards Bedlam, the Zork series and the Spellcasting series.

There are opportunities for writers to write the scripts for this type of graphic fiction but I'm not sure how much money you would make, if any. A great site for getting started though is Playfic (www.playfic.com), an online community, which helps you to write and share your interactive fiction. It has tutorials to help you as you progress along the way to being an interactive fiction writer.

Collaborative Fiction

Collaborative fiction is a body of work produced by a group of writers. They take turns writing chapters or being responsible for one character or subplot that runs throughout the story. This type of fiction has a growing following on the Internet as its global nature makes it far easier for writers from anywhere in the world to work together.

One recent project produced a story page by page. You read the previous page and submit the next page of the story. The editor chooses which page is the best to continue the story on and the process is repeated each day until the story ends, using many writers to create a work of fiction. The website, Storymash (www.storymash.com), works in a similar way but uses different writers to create a book chapter by chapter. They actually pay writers for each chapter they write so if you feel like trying your hand at collaborative fiction, you could give it a go!

Collaborative fiction is great fun to try out and puts you in contact with so many other writers. The only downside is that if the book you all work on does go to print, it could run into legal complications with so many writers demanding their share of the rights. Splitting royalties between say fifty writers would be a nightmare and each would earn very little.

Yet sites like Protagonize (www.protagonize.com) have over 20,000 members. They showcase a range of fiction including 'addventures'. Addventures are stories where you choose your own adventure by clicking on various options or links. They are a form of hypertext fiction which tells a story through branching out into different segments rather than a having a linear structure. Do you remember those fantasy books where you got to choose the next part of the story by turning to a different page? These are just like that but online. Look at their site for examples of a range of online fiction and check out their great FAQs section that answers a range of queries.

To get a feel for collaborative fiction in a range of genres and styles, Goodreads (www.goodreads.com), has a list of around 42 books that have been made as part of a collaborative or round-robin process. Make your own mind up whether these have worked or whether they seem disjointed by reading a few different types.

Hypertext Fiction

Hypertext stories include links that move you from one part of a story to another. Addventures are one form of hypertext fiction but there are other types of stories that use this format. A selection can be found at 101: One Zero One, a hypertext fiction site, at They include stories, poems, art and films on their site.

A hypertext story evolves through a choice of links whether textual or graphic and the user is in control of a story that has many possibilities and paths to take. It is also used for hypertext poetry where at the click of a button, new sentences can be added and a completely new poem created.

The story or poem that you create, however, is not yours. It was written by someone else and so the end result is not something that you could use as your own work. Hypertext writers who can build a story from scratch are in demand. The website, Eastgate (www.eastgate.com), showcases stories and also provides tools you can use to build your own hypertext narratives. You will need a certain level of computer knowledge to navigate your way around creating a hypertext work of fiction but if you love fiction writing and are up for a challenge, then this could be what you are looking for.

Poetry on the Web

Poetry has really come into its own on the web. To date, it has been notoriously difficult for poets to see their work in print form. Poetry magazines are few and far between and book submissions of first time poets are rarely published. The Internet has given beginners and established poets a chance to show off their work to a worldwide audience.

The Internet has also changed poetry and the forms it can take. Although what we would class as 'normal' poems appear on many websites, digital poetry has also developed with poems becoming more artistic with moving words, 3D patterns and all amount of visuals and graphic tricks to bring a poem to life.

As in the publishing world, poetry will not make you a millionaire and I've yet to find a site that pays poets a good rate for their work. However, some sites like Poetry (www.poetry.com), do link you to a community of millions that will read and review your work, giving you almost instant feedback on whether your poem is a masterpiece or needs improving. Poem Online (www.poetry.org) is similar in that it is an online community of poets that aim to help poets hone their craft. You can get honest feedback on your work from other poets using this site and then post your final draft on their blog.

The Internet Poets Co-operative is a site where you can share your work via their forums or chat to other poets in their 'virtual coffeehouse'. Their site, has loads of poetry to listen to via free MP3 downloads or you can read their poetry books online. The website of The Academy of America Poets (www.poets.org) is also packed with resources including poems, biographies of poets and locations of poets near you (in the US). Finally, if you are looking for help with your poetry, All Poetry (www.allpoetry.com) has free classes so that you can practice your skills before unleashing them on the World Wide Web.

Comments and Feedback

When you post your story, novel or poem on the web, you will often receive feedback, comments and criticism. Readers are often encouraged to say whether they liked your story and would recommend it to other people. This is a great way for you to find out whether your writing works and what your readers like or dislike about it.

If you are considering using the characters in your short story to form a full length novel, this feedback can help you to decide if it's worth pursuing and the comments your readers make can help you to develop the plot and characters in a way that you know your readers will like. In the same way, a serialised novel with great feedback will show whether it has the potential to be sent to a mainstream publisher.

Of course, there will be days when the criticism is not so constructive and people can and will post disparaging comments on websites when they have nothing better to do. Ignore the negatives and focus on the positives. The positive comments will be from readers who are looking forward to reading more of your work. Once you have built up an audience, keep them satisfied with more and more of your writing.

Fiction Competitions

There are many poetry and fiction competitions online. They vary in prizes given and the cost of the entry fee. Some are free; others are $30 or more. Some can lead to publication and if nothing else, will get you working to a deadline. Here are a few worth looking up:

- Fish Publishing (www.fishpublishing.com) run a yearly flash fiction competition with a €1,000 first prize and inclusion in one of the Fish anthologies.
- The Annual Interactive Fiction Competition (www.if comp.org) has been running an Interactive Fiction competition for over 17 years. Their prizes are donated and can be absolutely anything from chocolates to a tarot reading!
- Flash 500 (www.flash500.com) have a quarterly themed competition for flash fiction with a first prize of £300 and publication in Words with Jam.
- The Dublin Review of Books (www.drb.ie) has a new flash fiction competition with a great €1,000 first prize. Submissions are accepted online or by email. Entry fee is €10.
- First Writer (www.firstwriter.com) runs an online short story competition. You are invited to send in up to 5 stories not exceeding 3,000 words. They can be on any subject and in any genre. First prize is £200.

- Wordstock Festival (www.wordstockfestival.com) is Portland, Oregon's festival of books, writers and story-telling. They have an online short story competition for stories between 1,500 - 3,000 words with a first prize of $1,000. The top ten writers' work will be published in 'The Woodstock Ten' anthology available at the festival and other outlets.
- Ink Tears (www.inktears.com) run flash fiction and short story competitions and winning entries are published on the website including the author's biography. The entry fee is £3 and first prize is around £300.
- Fan Story (www.fanstory.com) is an online community for writers that supports loads of competitions throughout the year - fiction and poetry. It's free to join and enter their competitions which all have prizes. Everything contributed also gets feedback and constructive comments.

The Great NaNoWriMo

NaNoWriMo stands for the National Novel Writing Month although it is now an international event. It started in America and has now gone global. Every November writers are challenged to write a 50,000 novel in 30 days. You can write in any genre and about anything. You don't have to be a great writer; you just have to complete the word count. Once completed and submitted before the deadline, you have won.

Winning means not much more than the fact that you can say that you've done it although you will receive a certificate and have your name on the Winner's Page. But how many writers can say they produced a novel in 30 days? There are some other bonuses like being able to purchase writers' software at discounted prices or having a direct line to a printer. But you also have a manuscript that is ready to be worked on.

I could say that you'd have a novel ready to be published but honestly if you have written 50,000 words in a month, your work will need serious editing. Just achieving that word count means that you won't have been able to edit as you go along and have had time to consider other ways in which your novel could work or be improved upon.

Still, you have 50,000 words and that is the basis of a novel. You can spend the rest of the year making your novel book publisher ready or start preparing it to be published as an e-book. To have a working manuscript in such a short space of time is a great boost to your confidence. Just knowing that you can write a novel can lead you on to better and brighter things.

NaNoWriMo has also turned into a global writing community. It has a huge following from all around the world and there are forums which allow you to connect to other writers involved in the project. It can turn quite competitive amongst writers who set themselves a daily word count and tweet regularly how well they are doing. But there are others that it doesn't come as easy to and there is amazing support for anyone taking part.

There is also physical support with Nano Near You which lets you know of any events or groups that are taking part in your own locality. Check out their website to see if there is a writing group near you.

Chapter Five

Research and Information

Every writer will need to research elements of their writing whether they are writing fiction or non-fiction. Facts need to be checked, new information brought to light and archives delved into for accuracy when writing all kinds of descriptions and settings. The Internet is a mine of all information (and dis-information!) that can be utilised to support your work.

Why use the Internet for Research?

I think it's safe to say that writers love books. My collection has grown over the years and changed with whatever type of writing I've been focusing on. There're social science tomes, self-help guides, psychology textbooks, historical non-fiction, website design books, writers' guides, the list goes on... they cover every shelf in my office and there's little space for anything else!

I've regularly purchased books when I've had a piece of writing to research but sometimes at more of a cost than I've actually made from the writing. The joy of being able to conduct research on the Internet is that for the most part, it is free. I'll never stop collecting books but by using the Internet, I can keep the costs down and only buy books that are essential. I can also choose to write about subjects that I wouldn't have otherwise considered because a wealth of information is available to me in a short space of search time.

If you have a good Internet connection then researching can be a far quicker option than waiting on the mailman or a courier to deliver a long awaited order. There are also the benefits of being able to retrieve material that you wouldn't have ordinarily been able to access. Documents, academic papers, company reports, product information, and archived material can be sourced to add much more detail to your writing. Whether you write fiction or non-fiction, the Internet is a resource that is just waiting to be used.

Using the Internet for Research

The Internet is a super fast way of researching even the smallest details in your writing. Whether it's checking spellings, place names, dates or events, it's all there at the click of a mouse. I have Google running in the background whenever I'm writing an article and when I need to check out something I'm not one hundred per cent sure of, I search for more information.

There are millions of sites on thousands of subjects throughout the Internet and it's easy to get lost in the never-ending stream of web pages. Using the Internet for research means knowing what you are looking for and going after it by using directories, archives and sites that are specific to your writing interests. The more you become familiar with which websites give you the best information, the more you will head straight to them for your answers.

The problem with the Internet is that it throws out all sorts of information at you and it's not all necessarily correct. The World Wide Web is not regulated. There is no-one checking the content of websites to make sure they are accurate and credible. Anyone can have a website and post anything on it. So when you are doing your research, you need to make sure that your information is coming from a reliable source.

Double-checking your Facts

Double-checking the facts you find on the Internet is essential. There are just too many mistakes and unintentional errors on the World Wide Web for any one page to be taken as the absolute truth. While there are many authoritative and informative sites out there, no writer should ever assume that the facts they find are correct. There is nothing worse than having an article published and someone calling the editor to say that it was rubbish. Worse, that it's completely untrue. It undermines your credibility as a writer and will make an editor think twice about using your work again.

However, you can easily double-check your facts by cross-referencing. Say you find the date of an event on one website, you can then check on two or three other sites to ensure that that date is correct. By matching your facts up with the facts on other sites, you will see whether a website is right or whether the information has been misused.

One tip is to browse official sites rather than sites that volunteers have added to. For instance, a website that belongs to a civil war historical association will be more reliable than a website that just has general civil war articles. Or a university psychology site that is written by professors will contain more expert knowledge than a psychology chat forum used by students. Look at who is writing for the site and check out their credentials. It will give you an idea of whether the site contains information from reputable sources.

Organising your Research

As I mentioned before, the curse of the constant browser can mean you spend hours on the Internet with little to show for it. Always know what you are looking for before you start. Make a list of the queries you have or the websites you know that you want to look at. Cross them off as you go along and mark any new links you want to follow. But give yourself a time limit or set aside a certain time that is just for research.

I tend to use Friday afternoons' as research time. I write all week then research the next stage of my writing ready for use come Monday morning. Find a time that suits you that will support your work instead of encroaching into your precious writing time.

There are many ways to organise your research. You can

bookmark pages or use software like One Note to save information you have found. I tend to use the old-fashioned way of keeping a notebook with the websites I have used and noting what they are good for. If I know that I will need to read over what I have found, I'll print it off and mark on paper the website, date and time I have found it. These are then stored in an A-Z file for future use.

This may seem like a waste of paper but it is surprising how quickly websites close down or articles that were posted disappear into the cosmos. I once wrote a series of articles that served as great links to show editors when I was looking for more work. The website company changed hands and none of the original articles were kept online. I hadn't printed them out and so lost a valuable body of work to show prospective clients.

You can also cut and paste relevant information into a Word document and include the website link for future reference. For instance, when I was looking at the history of the Internet, I looked at several sites, cut and pasted their most important information and then went through the document I had created for consistencies, picking out the most relevant facts for the purpose of this book. You can also save entire web pages to read through when you are offline rather than printing off reams of paper.

Information Gathering by Email

One way to check your facts is to contact the writer of information displayed on a web site directly. I like to think that interviewing by email is like checking with a reliable source although many journalists would tell you otherwise. For the purposes of my writing, interviewing by email has been a valuable way of getting in touch with a professional or expert, who otherwise would not have the time to meet face-to-face or lives so far away as to make travel impossible.

Many experts are willing to partake in interviews by email especially if they are going to be quoted or mentioned in an article or acknowledged in a book. Emails, by design, are usually short and sweet. You don't want to be sending a list of 50 questions that will be too time-consuming for your interviewee to answer. Decide on the top 10 questions that will provide answers that can be used in your writing; if you can narrow it down to five, all the better. You can always ask for more information at a later stage.

Send a preliminary email to your chosen professional outlining why you would like to interview them, what it is that you are researching and the purpose of your research. Include a brief biography of yourself so that they have a sense of who you are. You can add one or two links to previous work if you think that it will help your approach.

Once they have agreed to an interview by email, send out your questions making sure that they are open questions, the type that encourages a detailed answer. It's a waste of your time and theirs to use closed questions that can be answered with a simple yes or no. Think of what information you really need from the interview and ask questions that will give you the details and facts that will make all the difference to your writing.

Always send a thank you email after the interview - you never know when you may need their help again! When your work is published, send them a copy or a link to your writing if it is online.

Web Directories

There are different types of websites that you can use to conduct your research. Web directories are sites that compile lists of more sites for you to visit in a particular subject area. Instead of just using your browsers' search facility, you can go to a web directory that will have categorised sites that you can link directly into. Web directories are free to use and can cut out hours of browsing time by getting you to the most relevant sites.

Some I have used are:

- Best of the Web Directory: www.botw.org
- The Open Directory Project: www.dmoz.org
- Webotopia: www.webotopia.org
- Exact Seek: www.exactseek.com

Article Directories

Article directories are sites that contain a collection of articles categorised by subject area. There are often opportunities to write for such sites but they are usually unpaid. This type of directory contains short articles of around 500 words that have been posted by the author. The sites will only take unique content but that doesn't mean that they are factually correct. These articles will still need double-checking if you are using them for reference.

However, if you are considering writing articles for the web, you can use these sites to check what else has been written in your subject so that when you write a new article, you know that it is original. You can also use these sites to post your work and to build up your own portfolio.

Look up sites such as:

- Ezine Articles: www.ezinearticles.com
- Article Alley: www.articlealley.com
- Buzzle: www.buzzle.com
- Go Articles: www.goarticles.com
- Helium: www.helium.com
- Amazines: www.amazines.com
- About: www.about.com

Reference Sites

Oh, how I love to browse Wikipedia! It's my first port of call when needing some basic info on an event, person or place. It's easy to search, free to use and each entry has links to further information that can take you off on many a tangent. However, not all the articles are verified so any facts that you glean from the pages do need double-checking.

Another great site is Britannica Online. Remember those old dusty encyclopaedias that were collected and displayed on many a bookshelf? They have an online version that is free for an initial trial period and you can subscribe at a low cost thereafter.

Reference sites do vary as to whether they are free or require some sort of subscription charge. Some of the best free sites include:

- Reference: www.reference.com
- Encyclopedia: www.encyclopedia.com
- About: www.about.com
- Refdesk: www.refdesk.com

These can be a real help when you just need basic facts to complement your writing or are looking for some background information before researching a subject in greater depth.

Specialist Websites

The more you browse your specific interests, the more you will find sites that specialise in your field. For instance, if you enjoy writing personal growth and self-help articles, you might regularly log onto Worldwide Health (www.worldwide health.com) or Self Growth (www.selfgrowth.com). Interested in the car industry? Then Automotive Digest (www.automo-tivedigest.com) or Auto News (www.autonews.com) can keep you up-to-date with the latest developments. What about organic gardening? Organic Gardening (www.organicgardening.com) and Organic Gardening Information (www.organicgar-deninginfo.com) share all the latest gardening tips and advice. Whatever area you like to write in, there are websites that can keep you informed and provide great research for your own writing.

Having a list of sites that you regularly visit can keep you informed about the latest changes, trends and developments in any area you are interested in writing about. Even if you are a fiction writer, you can keep in touch with fiction writers' associations, book publishers and market trends by keeping an eye on the sites most relevant to you. Sign up for any newsletters that are offered to receive news by email. If they start to flood your inbox or they aren't really relevant, you can always unsubscribe from their mailing list.

Genealogy Sites

I have written about the use of ancestry and genealogy sites in my previous book, *Telling Life's Tales: Writing Life Stories for Print and Publication*. Genealogy sites are great for researching family history or for finding out more about people you wish to write about but they can also be a good resource for researching other elements of people's lives.

Old census records can be used to find out typical names and surnames from a certain era or the occupations that were popular at the time. If you are writing about a particular locality, you will find lists of the families that lived there when the census was recorded. Military records give a sense of who a soldier was and what battles he fought in. Emigration records give details that can be used to flesh out characters in stories and novels. As well as dabbling in your own family research, you can use genealogy websites to add detail to your writing.

Try browsing sites like Find My Past (www.findmypast.com), Genuki (www.genuki.org.uk) and Ancestry (www.ancestry .co.uk) for British family information and Roots Web (www.rootsweb.com), Cyndi's List (www.cyndislist.com) and Olive Tree Genealogy (www.olivetreegenealogy.com/usa) for American research.

Online Libraries

Of course, your local library may have an online facility and if they do it's a great way of ordering books to aid your research but in this case, by online libraries, I mean collections of a vast array of material that can be located and downloaded from the Internet. When I was studying for my degree, I used libraries such as Questia to find material for literature reviews, to provide quotes and to lend credence to any theories I was discussing. As a student, access was free to various academic libraries online. For writers looking at academic libraries, the costs can be high but if you regularly write in-depth articles or books in one particular subject area, a basic subscription will provide you with huge amounts for material for reference purposes.

Archives

Some online archives are free and easy to use. They contain a wealth of materials from documents and newspapers to historical research papers and compiled records. Archive . archive.org) is a general archive website with links to many resources. A lot of universities and institutes also provide archives that are easily accessible online. Archives Hub (www.archiveshub.ac.uk) is a website with archives covering science, technology, health, the arts and humanities, plus other subjects. It has been added to by nearly 200 institutions across England, Scotland and Wales to make a vast array of information available to the general public. The National Academies Press (www.nap.edu) was created by the National Academies in the USA to publish the reports issued by the National Academy of Sciences, the National Academy of Engineering, the Institute of Medicine, and the National Research Council. They have a huge range of PDF files that can be downloaded that cover the subject areas of science, engineering and medicine.

Archives can be very specific like the Internet Library of Early Journals, (www.bodley.ox.ac.uk), a collection of key British journals from the 18th and 19th centuries. Often this kind of archive was compiled due to a university research project and they can be extremely valuable when conducting your own research.

Look at what some archive sites have to offer when you are researching your own work. They often contain unusual and interesting documents that you can use to add colour to your writing.

Free E-Books

Who doesn't love a free book? When you are researching you often need to read a little of a lot of books to give yourself a general understanding of the event or place you are writing about. To go out and buy all your research books can be extremely expensive and if your library doesn't stock what you want or they take too long to find you a book, then free downloadable books through the Internet could be the answer.

Project Gutenberg (www.gutenberg.org) has provided me with many free research books taken from their collection of over 40,000 books. They provide access to one of the oldest digital libraries in a range of formats. The books are also available on CD and DVD so you can have a ready-made digital collection to use on your computer whenever you need it.

Downloading e-books means that you will either need to read them via your computer or an e-reader device like the Kindle. These can be bought relatively cheaply now and electronic devices like the iPad make access even easier.

There are two types of free e-books; the old classics and newly published works. Sites like Project Gutenberg and Free Books (www.freebooks.com) provide classical stories by authors such as Jane Austen, Charles Dickens, Lewis Carroll, James Joyce and many more. Other sites, like Free E-books (www.free-ebooks.net), concentrate more on new writers covering a range of subjects. They are also open to submissions and although you don't actually sell your work, you can build your fan-base and earn revenue from their ad scheme.

Doing your Market Research

This type of research is different from the checking of facts and information for inclusion in your writing. This is the research you need to do before you write! Market research for writers is all about knowing where you are going to send your work to.

For web writers, that means searching the Internet for opportunities and websites to work for. For fiction writers, it could mean browsing short story sites or book publishers. Whatever type of writing is your forte; the Internet can help you to decide what the best market opportunities are for you. Many print magazines have their own websites and they include writers' guidelines or submissions sections so you can check whether what you are writing is a good match. Book publishers also have detailed submissions sections and may list their requirements. Either way you can look to see what type of books they publish and whether your work would easily fit into their lists.

Using the Internet to check your market means that you will know what a magazine, website or publisher is looking for before you send in something that they really don't deal with. Once you know where you are going to send your work, you can start researching the other elements of your writing to make it the most amazing work an editor has yet to see!

Chapter Six

Education Online

As well as being a place for research, the Internet is also a place of education. There are many websites a writer can use to aid their development, learn new skills and support their writing endeavours. For established writers, there's also the possibility of being more involved in education by working as an online tutor or creating your own courses for other writers to participate in.

Courses for Writers

Whatever stage you are at in your writing career, there are courses available through the World Wide Web that will accommodate your level of ability. From beginners' level to degree level, there are courses aimed at improving your writing skills and helping you to develop into a published writer.

Taking a writing course can be a good way of trying out a new genre or different area of writing and receiving professional feedback on your work. I recently took an online scriptwriting course as I've always wanted to write a TV or film script. I'd read books about this type of writing but what I really wanted was someone to look at my ideas and stories to see if they had any potential. The course I took was really informative and has encouraged me to continue to develop my own scripts. Sometimes a little extra encouragement can boost your confidence to try out new writing opportunities.

It can sometimes be hard to decide which course is best for you or where you need to focus your studies. You know you want to do something but what? Some universities offer free taster courses that you can use to update your skills as a standalone course or before studying an area of writing in greater depth:

- The Open University (www.open.ac.uk) has courses in Essay Writing, Descriptive Writing and Fiction Writing accessed through their OpenLearn web site.
- Purdue University (www.owl.english.purdue.edu) offer over 200 free resources for writers including courses in the Pattern and Variation in Poetry, Professional and Technical Writing and Proofreading Your Writing through their Online Writing Lab (OWL). The OWL website offers free advice, grammar and usage support plus one-to-one help from tutors.
- The News University (www.newsu.org) offers an e-learning programme for budding journalists. There are hundreds of courses with a technical or web focus including Writing Better Headlines, The Writing Process and Cleaning Your Copy.
- Massachusetts Institute of Technology (www.mit.edu) has free courses including Writing and Reading Short Stories, Writing and Reading the Essay and Writing and Reading Poems. They are all available through their OpenCourseWare (OCW) initiative.
- E-Zine University (www.ezineuniversity.com) has several courses to help you produce your own e-zines. In their content development and writing section, they have some courses like Writing Clearly and Effectively, Conquering Confusing Words and Quick Ways to Clean Up Your Writing that will benefit writers of all genres.

Some other educational courses can be found at no cost on the Internet. Creative Writing Now (www.creative-writing-now.com) offers fee paying courses but always has a short freebie you can try out. Writers Reign (www.writer sreign.co.uk) has free creative writing and article writing courses. The Writer's Helper (www.writers helper.com) offers Writing Verse for Children, Writing for the Web, and Make Your Price Sell at no charge.

There are other companies who specifically tutor writers for a fee. The Writers Academy (www.thewritersacademy.net) offer starter courses in areas such as freelance writing, creative writing and short story writing. Writers Online (www.writers-online.co.uk) also have poetry, scriptwriting and polishing your writing style courses. The Big Smoke Writing Factory (www.bigsmokewritingfactory.com) has courses like Starting a Novel, An Introduction to Writing Memoir and An Introduction to Writing Children's Fiction. Although not strictly 'online', these courses can be completed by email tuition with an experienced tutor. The joy of taking a course by email is that there is a much quicker turnaround on your work and you therefore receive good feedback before continuing your studies; whereas paper courses can take weeks to be marked, an online or email course will be marked in days and sometimes even hours. Writers anxious to get expert feedback on their work have found online and email courses to be more immediate to their needs.

For writers wishing to study to degree level, the Open College of Arts (www.oca-uk.com) has distance learning modules that can be taken to gain credits for a BA degree in Creative Writing. Modules include Writing Skills, Poetry, Lifewriting and Writing for Children.

The London School of Journalism (www.lsj.org) offers an online postgraduate diploma course in Journalism. All lectures, tutorials and group discussions take place online with start dates in February and September.

Of course, there are writers' courses that you can physically attend and some writers prefer to mix with groups of other students when they are learning new skills. Other writers prefer to learn from the comfort of their own home and may not have the time to go out to evening classes or return to college. If that sounds like you, online courses can be taken at a time that suits you and you can learn at your own pace.

Do You Know What Type of Learner You Are?

Before you embark on a course, it might be helpful to know what type of learner you are. The VARK system is a way of categorising learning styles. VARK stands for Visual, Aural, Reading (& Writing) and Kinaesthetic. You can test yourself online at VARK Learning (www.vark-learning.com) to find out your learning preferences. The relevance of knowing what learning style you have makes you more aware of how you absorb information. This will help you to focus your studies and will support you as a writer. Take the test to find out if you are multi-modal or if you favour a particular style.

Courses usually come in print or text format but due to the use of new technologies, other media now support many educational materials. They may have video clips to watch, audio files to listen to or interactive quizzes to take part in online. Pick a course that speaks to your strengths and will interest you as the type of learner you are. As well as helping you to pick a course that is right for you, knowledge of your VARK preferences can help you as a writer and the Internet can provide you with the extra resources you may need to support your learning style and the way you absorb information.

Visual writers absorb information from what they see. If this is you, you will need to support your writing by seeing images, pictures and graphics. When it comes to writing, visualising your story or novel will help so day-dreaming does have a purpose! Use the Internet to look at photos, maps and illustrations to help you visualise what you are writing about. Watch video clips on websites like YouTube or Vimio and search online TV archives for footage that will give you information visually.

Aural writers need to hear things that are relevant to their writing; download podcasts or MP files from the Internet that you can listen to whilst you write. If you have characters singing in a bar, listen to modern background music or karaoke tunes. If you are writing a story set in medieval times, listen to madrigals or lute melodies. Story set in a busy city? Then listen to the background noise of a city to help you to feel what it would really be like to live there. Help yourself to set your scenes by aural stimulation.

A reading and writing style means you absorb information well from the written word. You can use the Internet to find printed research materials and look into online archives and libraries for inspiration. You will feel comfortable reading through large swatches of information which you will definitely find when you start browsing!

Kinaesthetic writers need to touch and feel. This is one area where the Internet isn't overly useful but you can use it to find out where you can go and what you can do to give yourself kinaesthetic experiences. Find out where you could ride a horse, walk on a beach, or go up in a hot air balloon. Putting yourself in your characters' positions will help you to write about them with good authority. If you can experience what they will experience in your writing then it will make them much more believable and likeable to your readers.

Checking Out Your Course

Before you hand over your precious cash, check out the writing college that is offering online or email courses. As with research and information on the Net, you can never be sure of the quality and accuracy of the material without double-checking. To make sure that a company is legitimate and will offer you a good service, find out about:

- The quality of their materials - ask for a preview of course materials.
- Who are the tutors? - find out who your tutor is going to be and ask for their biography. They should be published writers and experts in their own genres.
- How much feedback will you get? - find out if your work

will get a full proof-read, comments and advice or just tips for future writing.

- Will they give you market advice? - tutors might be able to give you valuable tips on where to send your work.
- Have other students gone on to bigger and better things? - they might include students' feedback on their website but you can also ask if students have gone on to have work published or what the colleges success stories are.

Using Online Dictionaries and Thesaurus sites

Money tight? Then educate yourself on the Net. You can use the Internet to support your writing by using online facilities such as dictionaries and thesauri. Dictionary sites often include extras such as word games, crosswords and translation services. They are easy to dip into during your writing sessions but make sure you don't go off on a tangent and spend the day playing instead of writing!

- Your Dictionary (www.yourdictionary.com) is an easy to use site that also has computer, business, legal, medical and scientific dictionaries available.
- Oxford Dictionaries (www.oxforddictionairies.com) allows you to choose between British and American language searches.
- Merriam Webster (www.merriam-webster.com) is a US dictionary with an online Spanish/ English dictionary as well as word quizzes and a thesaurus.
- Dictionary Reference (www.dictionary.reference.com) is a packed site with a daily crossword, word of the day and crossword solver functions. They also host Thesaurus (www.thesaurus.com).
- Thesaurus (www.thesaurus.net) is a basic but functional site for your word needs.
- Collins Dictionary (www.collinsdictionary.com) has a great

English thesaurus facility and you can also suggest new words for their dictionary.

- Roget's Thesaurus can be found at www.education.yahoo.com and has over 260,000 synonyms listed.
- Check out the Dictionary of Slang (www.dictionaryofslang.co.uk) for info on British vernacular words.

Translation

You might never need to translate your work or that of others but translation sites can be useful if you do. I like to attempt to read a book written in the French language on occasion and when I do, I always need to translate words or passages of text. I do have a trusty dictionary but if you have large amounts of text that you don't understand, it's just so easy to type them in and get an online translation in seconds.

Some of the dictionary sites I have mentioned offer basic translation services but I have also used Babelfish . babelfish.com). This site translates French to English and the reverse as well as having other languages available such as German, Hindi, Arabic, Dutch plus others. It offers a mechanical translation which is free as well as a manual translation for which there is a charge. Another site I found recently when trying to write a letter in French is offered by Bing . bing.com/translator). Bing offer a free translation service for online automatic translation of text and web pages and it's good. I not only wrote my letter but I also translated passages of text very quickly. If you need to dabble in translation, look for sites that are easy to use and have the languages of your choice.

Checking your Grammar

Even the best of us have to check our grammar usage at times. Whilst you might not want to keep checking during writing sessions, when you reach the editing stage, part of the process is to make sure your work is grammatically correct. It also never hurts to brush up on your grammar every now and again. You may think you know all you need to know but I bet when you look at one of these websites you'll find out something new!

Grammar Book (www.grammarbook.com) is a free online English usage website that includes grammar rules on the use of pronouns, verb agreements, punctuation rules and commonly confused words plus quizzes to test your knowledge. Daily Grammar (www.dailygrammar.com) is advertised as a website for school-going children or those that are home-schooled but also adults who need to brush up on their grammar skills. They have over 440 lessons and 88 quizzes for you to work your way through! Grammarly (www.grammarly.com) is a basic, easy to use online handbook but they also have software that can be downloaded to help you check your own work for grammatical errors.

If all this sounds too much like hard work, you can allow yourself to play some word games after you've brushed up on your skills. Learn a lot and play a little!

Just for Fun

Whilst my teenage sons use YouTube, social media and gaming websites for fun, I like to find word quizzes, spelling tests and crosswords for online relaxation. As well as filling a winter's evening, they can be educational as well as fun. Fun with Words (www.fun-with-words.com) is a dated looking website but it has some great puzzles to play including rebus word puzzles, boggle and hangman (I know - how old is that?!). They also have word puzzles like palindromes, spoonerisms and tongue twisters to work your way through. You can add your own too.

Shockwave (www.shockwave.com) is a much more modern site that has a host of games available including Super Text Twist, Word Roundup Challenge, Whizz Words and Prose and Motion. My most favourite game though, lame as it is, has to be 'Zombie Typocalypse' found on Word Games (www.wordgames.com). As you type in words, your spellings kill zombies and it gets faster and faster - purely addictive. This site has many well executed games from word searches to typing tests to keep you amused if you want to have fun with words.

Just remember to set aside a time for the fun part! It's so easy to start playing and realise you've lost an hour or two. Saying that all writers need some light relief at times so go and kill a few zombies - at least it will improve your typing speed!

Finding Writing Guidelines

In the last chapter, we talked about market research and finding out about writers' guidelines from magazines and publishers so that you can make sure your work fits their requirements before you submit any of your own writing. There are also sites for writers that have general writing guidelines that can give you tips and suggestions on how to improve your work.

The Eclectic Writer (www.eclectics.com) is a US site with a selection of informative articles on everything from characters and settings to writing a synopsis. The Author Network (www.author-network.com) is a site packed full of information for writers and has a good selection of advice giving articles. One of my favourite sites for all things to do with writing comes from Writers Digest (www.writersdigest.com), the providers of the US magazine of the same name. Their website has lots of guidelines, information and up-to-date articles to help writers learn more about their craft.

As you browse the different writing websites, you will find lots of information, help and guidelines to assist you in every element of the writing business. Search general sites for tips on the writing craft and more specific sites, for genre based information.

Working as an Online Tutor

For writers who already have an amount of experience and some published works under their belt, working as an online tutor can be a great way of passing on your skills and earning a little cash.

Jobs as an online tutor come up with writing colleges, universities and other course providers that include creative writing, journalism or other types of writing course. Look at their vacancy sections to see if they are advertising any positions. Failing that, send in your CV with a covering letter explaining what courses you would like to tutor. They just might keep you on file for when such a vacancy arises.

Do you have to have a good knowledge of computers to be an online tutor? Yes and no. I have worked for a college that emailed out their courses to students and their assignments were then emailed on to me. I corrected them and sent them back with feedback and comments for future writing as well as market advice. Another college I worked for had a similar system but with much more paperwork to fill out for each assignment, an online forum for students and tutors to chat, and an interactive site for students to test their knowledge. Any college using new technologies like Moodle should offer their tutors training or online support in using their forums or chat rooms. With a little practice, you'll be able to use their systems and communicate with students across the World Wide Web.

Tutoring is a great way to pass on your skills and to give advice to new writers whatever level they are at. For some tutoring positions, you will need a degree in a related discipline like English or Creative Writing, especially if the courses are being offered by a university. Other colleges will just want to see your biography, know more about your level of writing experience and whether you have been published. Spend some time on your CV before emailing it to prospective employers to make sure it reflects your writing experience.

Creating your Own Courses

If you can't find tutoring positions or you have an amazing idea for a new course for writers then why not create your own? If you're happy with learning new computer skills, you can set up your own website and have them available across the World Wide Web. You will obviously have to start by writing a course which can take time and commitment. You might also want to supplement it with video or audio clips. Once you have the materials ready, you can upload them to your website so they are available for purchase (or offer them free of charge, if you wish!).

Your courses can be as simple as PDF files that students can download or as complicated as you like utilising new technologies. Whatever way you wish to present them, the materials should be of good quality, beneficial to students and contain some form of assignment and feedback structure.

If this all sounds too complicated, there are companies that can help you out. Open Beyond (www.openbeyond.com) offers a global support platform and services for people who want to share their knowledge and expertise. They can help you to create your own e-learning site and become an online tutor using your own materials. It might not be free but their prices are very reasonable. If you want to start your own writing college business, then this could be the way to go.

Chapter Seven

Forums and Networking

Making connections is part of being a writer. You may wish that you could sit in your ivory tower, typing away on a steam-punk computer, shut away from the outside world but writers really do need to interact. At some point, you are going to want people to read your work. You will want a publisher to print your manuscript and there'll be moments when you need advice and maybe support to get your manuscript finished. Networking on the Internet can help you to get in touch with other writers and professionals in the publishing world and you can chat until your heart's content on writing forums with other like-minded people.

Why use Social Media for Networking?

The simple answer is that it will connect you to people around the globe. These can be friends, colleagues, other writers, professionals in the publishing industry and people you don't know but who are eager to read your work or find out more about you.

Writing can be a solitary profession. You sit at home on the computer for days on end typing your stories, articles and that all important novel but when do you get to talk with other writers or people who can give you advice and tips or the heads up on new working opportunities? You might be lucky to have a writers' cafe or a writing group near you that gives you somewhere to meet with other writers but for many other wordsmiths, they write in isolation and their contact with other writers is limited. Social media then opens up a whole new world, a way of being in contact with people from all over the globe. Not only does it give you support and a sense of connectedness, it also opens you up to writers from other cultures and new ways of working.

The Top Networking Sites

The top social networking sites are currently Facebook, Twitter and LinkedIn. Some other sites such as Bebo, Friendster, Hi5 and MySpace are also really popular but have a younger demographic and an emphasis on entertainment and relationships. Writers need to use sites that attract other professionals and can be used to promote their work. Facebook, Twitter and LinkedIn can all be used for this purpose.

LinkedIn

LinkedIn is a network for professionals representing 170 industries and over 200 countries. With over 50 million users, this site is for the writer who wants to be linked with other professionals in the industry. You can search for people you know and ask them to connect with you or send invitations to users that LinkedIn suggest as per your occupation. Contacts are categorised into groups, for instance, networking groups, conference groups or professional groups. So if you say that your occupation is a writer, you will be offered connections with other writers, editors, authors and people working in the publishing industry.

When I started using this site, I had all of 5 people on my list from my home country. Within the space of only a couple of months, this had jumped to 50 and I'm now connected with people across the globe. It has been said that the Internet is a great leveller and that communication across the Net is more equal than if you were meeting face to face. This site demonstrates that in that you can be linked with a Fortune 500 executive or the managing director of a publishing company who usually wouldn't be available to meet with you. I have commissioning editors and publishing managers on my list of connections that I will definitely be in touch with!

The other amazing thing about this site is the possible job opportunities that may come up. I was contacted recently through LinkedIn and asked to write two articles, one for print and one for a website. I was happy to oblige and hope that my connections will continue to lead me down new paths. The more connections you have, the more opportunities may arise.

Facebook

Facebook is a global networking site where users can add friends to their pages, regularly updating their wall posts and talking by live chat. Although mainly social, it is being used far more to advertise businesses and for people to promote their work. There are over 350 million registered users and it is estimated that 150 million of these log in every day. Facebook users can join networks organised by region, school attended, city or workplace and they can also join active groups interested in particular subjects like writing, films, celebrities, music and products.

I began using Facebook years ago to keep in touch with relatives across the world but today I also have a writer's page. Check it out at Facebook pages are easy to put together and can link you to other writers or fans of your work across the globe. You can add in interesting links to publishers, writing groups and any of your work that is currently online. You can also link your page to Twitter so that what you write on Facebook is then tweeted. Two birds with one stone, I say.

Twitter

It took me awhile to get used to Twitter. But I've no followers, I wailed to my son. Just be patient, he said, people have to get to know you and I think that's what makes Twitter special. You read little bits of information, little slices of life that let you into another person's world (or them into yours). When you tweet, you are writing a message of not more than 140 characters long. It's not a lot and sometimes I find myself having to edit down my tweets. It's definitely good practice for writing tightly!

I use Twitter to let people know when I have a new article out or to chat about a piece of writing I am working on but I also love to follow authors I admire, and read to see what they have been up to. Authors like Trudi Canavan and Joanne Morris regularly tweet about their daily lives as well as aspects of being a writer.

All these social networks are free to join and registering only takes a few minutes. The time you spend on them will pay off in your connection to other writers and readers of your work. Don't underestimate the power of social networks. They really are a great tool for writers to use.

The Best Writers' Forums

Writers' forums are online communities for writers who use them to post up questions, discuss writing advice and exchange tips and advice. They are great for networking specifically with other writers, especially when you want help with writing in a particular genre or info about courses, events and workshops. Here are a few of the best on the Web.

- Writers Cafe (www.writerscafe.org) has loads to offer writers from free competitions to publisher listings but they also have a forum where writers communicate and can follow each others work. They also have the option of creating your own online writing group or joining those of others for specifically focused chat.
- The Writing Room (www.writingroom.com) has forums that concentrate on drama, horror, novel writing, sci-fi, poetry and short story writing. Their forums are used by a mixture of new writers, published authors and writing experts so there's lots of sound advice and information on offer. They too let you create your own writing group to talk with other writers about a particular piece of work or to chat with like-minded writers.
- The Writer's Digest Forum can be found on their main website at www.writersdigest.com. It's one of the largest

forums that encompasses all genres, self-publishing, tips and advice and story competition posts. I particularly like their success stories forum and the 'writer 's block party' for all those stuck in the moment!

- Absolute Write (www.absolutewrite.com) is a website with loads of forums to take part in. As well as the genres section, they also have discussions on grammar and syntax, research, book promotion and job opportunities.
- In Chapter Four, we talked about the NaNoWriMo, the National Novel Writing Month. They have a forum at for all writers participating in the 'write a novel in a month' competition. If you are thinking of giving this a go, then you can get extra support on a daily basis from others who are also taking part.
- Writers (www.writers.net) has four main categories on their forum; the writing craft, publishing and editing, genre based discussion and events. Although a small site, there is lots of information exchange between writers and you could pick up some useful tips here.
- Writers Weekly (www.writersweekly.com) is mostly for freelancers and focuses on jobs and paying markets. They also have a 'whispers and warnings' section for writers to tell others about companies they have worked for or websites that freelancers have had a negative experience with.

How to Use Them

The major networking sites like Facebook, Twitter and LinkedIn are all free to join and to create your own profile. They are easy to set up and you can give as little or as much information about yourself as you want. LinkedIn does have a premium service but I would suggest you become familiar with any site you are using before forking out your cash. Make sure you will continue to use it rather than it being a five minute wonder.

Google their web addresses and look for a log in or register section on their home page. Any of these sites takes just a few minutes of entering details before you are an active user. Once you have your profile up and running, you can connect with other people.

These sites all have different privacy policies so check them out before any of your information goes live. For instance, my family Facebook page is private but my writer's page is accessible to everyone. If someone new wants to look at your Facebook page, they have to send a friend request and then it's up to you whether you ok that. (You can always de-friend them after if you find they are posting strange messages on your wall!) With Twitter, you can follow people and companies who interest you and they can follow you too. Their tweets are listed on your home page whenever you log in. LinkedIn only allows you to link with people who accept your invitation to be connected. You can then access their profiles and see what they have been up to.

Once you have your own active profile on any of these websites, you are ready to start posting your messages to the world! How much you use these sites is up to you but be warned, Facebook especially, can become addictive and you'll find that you can spend hours changing your page, adding updates and talking to other people. I tend to post messages or tweets once or twice a week when I have a link to add or something new to say. It is possible to use them via your mobile phone but I'd never get any work done if I started that! We'll look more at how to use social networking sites for promotion purposes in Chapter Nine.

Netiquette

Netiquette is short for Internet etiquette. It's a social code for communicating across the World Wide Web. Talking to people over the Internet is a different experience from meeting someone face to face but the same rules of courtesy apply.

When talking to other writers try to be polite and considerate of other people's opinions. You will often find, when using forums, that you end up in a particular debate. Of course it's fine to have differing opinions but if you are abusive or find yourself typing out a rant, you may be banned by the website's administrator. Express your difference of opinion but in a polite manner. It'll definitely test your word skills!

Do not make personal comments or attack another person's piece of work. Using the Internet to connect with other writers is about open and positive communication and not making enemies the minute you start posting. If you know the person you are talking to be very careful about mentioning any of their personal information. Some forums are public and this means anyone can read the posts.

Make your writing as grammar, spelling and punctuation perfect as you can. There is a tendency for people to use text speak when using the Internet (I'm ashamed to say I've done it!) but when posting on writers' forums, you'll want to show that, well, you're a writer. Never use capital letters - it's like SHOUTING! Be yourself and maintain a level of honesty. You didn't really co-write Lord of the Rings, did you? Or had your fantasy idea stolen by J K Rowling? Boasting doesn't get you anywhere. It may not be face to face communication but other users will still not appreciate being lied to.

If you'd like to find out more about the conventions of Internet etiquette, there is a great book, *Netiquette* by Virginia Shea, that goes into some detail on how to communicate through the World Wide Web. It can give you more tips and advice on the conventions of writing when using the Internet.

Critique Groups

Many of the writing forums or websites for writers include some form of critiquing service. They may have one-to-one arrangements that you have to pay for but they may also have a free critique group where writers post their work and receive feedback from other writers and readers. These sites can give you an idea of where your writing works and where it needs improvement.

I recently decided to try out a new genre of writing and posted a children's story I was working on for critique. Feedback told me that one of the characters didn't feature enough in the run up to the ending for some readers. They had particularly taken to a sub-character and wanted to know more about him so that allowed me to go back through the editing process with the knowledge that this was one character that needed to stand out more. I could see it once I looked but if I hadn't had it pointed out to me, that poor character would have stayed unnoticed until the end.

Not all feedback that you receive will be positive so be prepared for comments that are disheartening. Try to understand why your work has been critiqued in such a way. Consider what you can do to improve your writing but remember at the end of the day, that if you feel that your writing is as good as it can be, then only an editor or publisher will make the final call on whether it's good enough to grace their lists. Critique sites are not there to discourage writers and you will find that most of the comments you receive will be constructive and informative. They may even lead you to a new market for your work.

- Writing (www.writing.com) is an online community that was set up in 2000 for writers of all interests and abilities. It's a great site for posting your work and receiving feedback from readers.
- My Writers Circle (www.mywriterscircle.com) is a forum type website where you can have your work critiqued but they also have specific forums for script writers and poets to have their work reviewed.

- Critique Circle (www.critiquecircle.com) is a free online collaborative writing workshop for all genres. It works by using a credit system. You earn credits by critiquing other peoples work and then can 'spend' yours by posting your own work. This web site has been highly recommended to me by other writers.
- The Desk Drawer (www.winebird.com) offers an email-based writing workshop, that sends out a weekly writing exercise. You can take part in a range of exercises to help you learn the craft of writing but you are required to submit at least three posts per month.
- Ladies Who Critique (www.ladieswhocritique.com) is a free critique partner matching site for writers of all levels. It's like a dating website, but instead of finding a new relationship, you are matched with a critique partner. You can use the site to search for partners based on their genre, their writing history and critiquing experience, allowing you to select who looks at your work.

Critiquing other Writers' Work

Rubbing your hands with glee, you might think oh yes, now I get my own back! Sorry, doesn't work like that! Although we might like to pull apart other people's work, when we use a critique site it's to give positive feedback and constructive criticism.

Why would you use a critique site? To get advice and pointers on what to improve in your own work. So if you are giving the feedback, that's what you want to pass onto others. It's about offering solutions to where someone may be going wrong.

If you are critiquing another writer 's work, start by commenting on the strength of their writing. What is good about it? What works well? Then go onto its weaknesses. What isn't working well? What needs changing? And then offer some solutions. Comment on what you would do to improve their writing. Offer support and encouragement because the last thing you want is to put someone off their writing for life.

You don't need to read through a manuscript like a proof-reader. If there are inconsistencies in grammar and punctuation, note them down and give an example, but don't rewrite the entire body of work for them. Read through their writing, jotting down notes, and then before you send in your comments, read through what you have said to make sure it is positive and constructive. Make sure that the critique you write is one that you would be happy to receive.

Being Careful

As you begin to use the Internet and most particularly, social networking sites and forums, you will find some writers who are happy to meet you - in the real world! We've all heard strange stories about Internet users going to meet someone they've met on the web and they turn out to be someone completely different. Being careful about first meetings is essential to protecting yourself.

Never give out your home address in your profile information and if you agree to meet with someone offline, make sure it is in a busy, public place and let your family or friends know where you are going. The chances are that if you agree to meet another writer, especially at a workshop or conference, they are going to be who they say they are. But you can never be too careful so take the necessary precautions before meeting online friends for the first time.

Chapter Eight

Publishing your own E-book

A few years ago, publishing your own book would have seen you using vanity or self publishers where you'd pay a fee to see your work in print. The event of the Internet has changed the publishing industry irrevocably and hailed the arrival of digital publishing where e-books can be uploaded directly from publishers and authors and downloaded by readers across the globe. They can then be read on a computer or downloaded to a Kindle or other e-reader device. The e-book has most definitely arrived.

What is an E-book?

An e-book is just a book in electronic form. That's it. It's still a book but it is in an electronic format and must be read with some kind of electronic device. This can be your computer but smaller devices, known as e-readers, are more common. E-readers come in all shapes and sizes from the extremely popular Kindle to the Nook tablet. You can also use your iPad or similar tablet device and even your mobile phone. The difference between all of these is whether the display is black and white, like the Kindle or some Sony readers, or a colour tablet-sized device like the iPad.

The key to purchasing an e-reader is to decide whether it's just for reading - the Kindle - or you want it to have computer like functions - the iPad. There are differences in size, weight and price. Choosing one that suits you is a matter of browsing the latest devices and deciding which one best accommodates your needs.

When they first came out, I had 'e-reader ' firmly underlined on my Christmas list. I so wanted one and chose a Sony PRS-300. I still have it and I've rarely used it but that's just me! My suggestion is that if you are shopping around for an e-reader; don't spend too much money on it until you know that that really is the way you are going to read books. I just can't drag myself away from good old print but my e-reader does have its uses.

And even if you don't want to read via an electronic device, millions of other people do so there is a market for your work that you can tap into by producing your own writing in an e-book format.

What's the Fuss all about?

Some people feel that the popularity of e-books will spell the end of print books. It's continually debated on writers' websites and in magazines and journals. There are arguments for and against both. E-books are lighter to use, print books are too heavy. E-readers can store thousands of books in one small package whereas you'd have to have a personal library if all your books were in print (I'd love that!).

I have to admit that I prefer print books (can you tell?) but I do have my trusty Sony e-reader for downloading freebies off the Net when I'm researching. I just don't feel comfortable curling up with one on the sofa, in the bath or in bed. My close friend, however, takes hers to bed every night. She swears by it. She can take her glasses off and adjust the screen to a larger font whilst having it propped on the duvet. Having a wireless version, if she gets bored with what she's reading, she just downloads something else.

People are divided over their use but e-books definitely have some advantages over print. E-books don't go 'out of print', the way a paperback would. They can be available indefinitely as long as the website they are advertised on stays up and running and even if that goes, it can be offered elsewhere.

Some e-book websites can also translate books so your work can be available to people around the world in their own language. If you were waiting for your print book to be available in other languages, it would be based on your sales and they may never be enough for your publisher to risk other editions.

The price of e-books has dropped and you can now buy new books at less than their print counterpart. Many classics can be downloaded for free and many first authors discount their books to a few pounds to increase their readership. It would be safe to say that e-books are cheaper in general to purchase unless you gather books at car boot sales and from charity shops (like me!).

If we look at the ecological side of e-books, we are talking less paper and no ink. Trees are saved by downloading e-books and there isn't the production of waste water from the process of pulping. Publishers aren't drumming up air miles shipping the books around the globe. There is some debate to the amounts of carbon emitted by e-readers and their use of electricity but all in all, e-books are more environmentally friendly.

And ultimately, they are easy to purchase. You don't have to physically go out and get them. You don't have to wait for your order to arrive in the post or by courier. They are with you within a few seconds or minutes, depending on your Internet connection, after you have purchased them.

The downside is they just don't have the appeal of a book book! Like I said you can't read them in the bath! There is just something so comforting about curling up on a rainy day with the book of your choice that an e-reader doesn't seem to offer. If you have children or grandchildren, sharing a print book at bedtime or looking at the pictures in a discovery book, can be a bonding experience. Ok, so you could use an e-reader but it's not the same as sharing a love of print books from an early age.

What about Christmas presents and the times when a book makes a great gift? I have spent a fortune over the past few years buying books as gifts, everything from annuals to how-to's and novels. I suppose you could download an e-book or buy an Amazon gift voucher but there is still something special about giving and receiving the present of a book.

You'll also never have to charge a print book! If the electric has gone and your e-reader is not charged, print is your only option. You can pick up a print book and just read it without worrying about the battery dying half way through your reading session. And print never fails. Technology always has glitches. Books get lost, files get corrupted and then the damn thing just won't work.

There are just so many pros and cons for both e-books and print and the above are just some of the arguments that are being talked about. One thing is certain and that is that the e-book is here to stay. They are a way in which writers can see their work published and become available to readers across the World Wide Web, no matter what side of the debate you are on.

The Benefits of Publishing your Work as an E-book

The main benefit of publishing your own e-book is that you are in control. You get to decide what goes on the cover, what price it retails at, what the word count is and when it will be available. You don't have to wait months for a publisher to get back to you nor do you have to go through a lengthy publishing process.

For a first time author, it can be a way of getting your work out there and gaining new readers. For other writers, it can be a way to try a new genre or of publishing novellas and anthologies. There are even some e-books that have been self-published that have led authors onto receiving a contract from a mainstream print publisher. If a publisher sees an e-book doing really well, there is the possibility that they will want to add it to their lists.

In the mainstream publishing industry where competition is high, you may never see your book accepted for print. Producing your own e-book means that you will see your work published even if only in electronic format so there will be an end result. Many writers never see their work published, for whatever reason, but with e-books, if you put the work in you know there will be a book at the end of it regardless of whether a main publisher takes it on or not.

Cost is a contributing factor. An e-book can be produced at little or no cost at all. That's in contrast to self-publishing. Even if you produced your own book on the printer at home you would have the cost of ink and paper. Using a self-publishing company could run into the hundreds but e-books? Next to nothing.

I produced my own e-book novella using free online PDF converter software and posted it on a website that was also free to use. It was sort of a trial run to see how easy it really can be. Sales have been small because I haven't put the effort needed into promoting it (more about promotion in the next chapter) but it proved that producing an e-book can be as simple or as complicated as you want it to be.

And you don't need a huge bunch of skills to go through the e-book process. It can be as simple as turning a Word document into a PDF file. This could be good for mini books or novellas that you want to offer from your own website. But to really gain sales, you want to embrace a process such as the one offered by Amazon and Kindle Direct Publishing. I'm not saying that selling your book on Amazon is the only way to go but I know it has worked for other writers, both in terms of ease of use and sales. Start by downloading their free e-book, *Building Your Book for Kindle*, for a user friendly guide to the process.

Preparing your Manuscript

So before we go any further, don't forget that your manuscript needs to be absolutely ready before you convert it into any other file type. As I've said PDFs are a typical file that is used by electronic devices but there are also others like .rtf and .html. Kindle Direct Publishing prefers a .prc format. Don't start panicking about formats! I know it might sound technical but PDFs are the most commonly used and KDP uses an easy conversion programme available from Mobipocket.

The thing is that once your file is converted, you can't do anything to change it so you need to make sure it is perfect before you start the process of turning your manuscript into an e-book. As a writer, you don't need me to tell you how you must edit, revise, review your work and cut, cut, cut until it is perfect. However, because your work is not going to go through a publisher 's editing process, you need to pay special attention to your grammar, spelling, punctuation and correct word usage. This is one time when it might be nice to pass your work onto family and friends to comment. They might be able to spot spelling errors and missed punctuation that you have passed over.

Remember you will also have to format your manuscript so that it looks like a book. Pick one off your shelf and you will see what I mean. Books have extra bits! A dedication page, a contents list, an index, perhaps a glossary or further reading section - it depends what type of book you are writing. You might also want to add in photos or images where appropriate but just remember that the more pictures you use, the larger the overall file size of the e-book will be. Readers might not want to download large files especially if they have a slow Internet connection. Once your manuscript is ready, add in any extra pages before formatting the whole thing. Here are some tips:

- Make sure that the body of your text is in a computer friendly font like Times New Roman throughout your manuscript.
- Set your page size to book size, either 6 x 9 or 5.5 x 8.5.
- Justify the text.
- Use single line spacing.
- Set your margins to not more than an inch on all sides.
- Set headers as per chapters if required.
- Add in page numbers when the manuscript is totally complete.

Once your manuscript is good to go, it's time to design your cover.

Cover Design

You can use Word to design the front cover of your book if you then convert it to a PDF document or there is a range of design software you can download to your computer, like Indesign. However you create your cover, it will need to include your title, subtitle (if any) and your name or the name that you will use as an author. Choose a background colour and then find an image that appropriately portrays the contents of your book.

There are some great online photograph websites to choose your pictures from. Some are free whilst others cost a small amount to download an image. Shutterstock.com, Flickr.com and Morguefile.com are well worth looking at for possible cover ideas.

The trick with designing a cover is to not overcrowd it. Keep it as simple as possible. Limit your use of colour so that your images and text stand out. Don't use more than two fonts for your text or it will begin to look cluttered and a bit like someone has gone design crazy!

Have a look at other e-book covers to see what works well and what doesn't. Especially look at how their covers portray genre. A murder mystery may have a knife or weapon on the front cover. A fantasy e-book may have a dragon or a fantastical landscape. A book about gardening will have an image of plants. Use your cover to say what your book is about before a browser has even read the title. Remember that the first time a potential buyer will see your book is as a small thumbnail in a list of e-books to purchase. It needs to stick out enough from the crowd to compel them to click on it for further details.

A Step-by-Step Process

So let's say you have a proofed manuscript and a cover that is good to go. To have your e-book available on Amazon, you can follow this step-by-step process. If you get stuck anywhere along the line, refer to the above mentioned Kindle e-book or use the help function on their website.

1 Begin by signing up to KDP at to open an account.
2 Enter all your book details including the title, a description, the language and your book categories.
3 Upload your book cover.
4 Upload your book file. You can upload a PDF file to KDP but they do prefer the .prc format. They recommend that you download the free Mobipocket Creator (www.mobi pocket.com) or use Kindlegen (www.amazon.com) if you are a MAC user. Both web sites contain guidelines on how to convert your files.
5 Choose your royalty rate.
6 Confirm your publishing territories.
7 Decide if you would like your book to be a part of Kindle's Book Lending scheme.
8 Save and publish your book.

Sounds easy? It is although you will be scratching your head from time to time and wondering what this or that means or how to do this or the other but their help section is top notch and will help you through each part of the process. Producing your first e-book will be a learning curve but once you've done it, there's nothing to stop you from doing it again and again!

How Much?

This can be hard to decide. Of course, you want to make money from your sales but if you are a first time author, will readers want to pay full price for your work? Many writers are selling their e-books for as little as 99 cents to entice more sales.

Purchasers may see it as a bargain and take the risk of not

knowing you as an author because the book price is minimal.

When you have decided where you are going to sell you work, look at the website to see how other authors have priced their books. This will give you an idea of what not to charge. There's no point in pricing your book at £7.99 if all the other books are under £5.

Take into account any royalty rates that you have to sign up to for placing your work on a website. Amazon has 75% and 35% rates so do a quick calculation to see what's best for you. E-books can also be susceptible to VAT so check with the website you are using as to whether you have to allow for a VAT payment in your purchase price. For instance, the UK charges 15% on digital books, Spain charges 22% and France 5.5%. It really does differ between countries so double-check any pricing information or help guides on the website you are using before finally settling on your e-book's price.

Where to Sell Your E-book

I have suggested that Amazon is a good website on which to have your book available but there are lots of other sites that will also host your book. Google ebooks, Barnes and Noble and Ebay all accept self-published e-books as do smaller companies like Smashwords, Bookyards and Lulu.

You can also set up your own website with a view to selling your e-books directly to your readers. It will mean that you will have to set up a payment function so that you can accept purchases. PayPal is easy to use and it's free to set up an account. I'll look at how you can use your own website for promotion in more detail in the next chapter.

Using an E-book Publisher

Of course, you can still send your book out to a mainstream publisher who may also publish your work as an e-book.

Likewise, there are new publishers springing up that only

deal with e-books. They accept your manuscript by email and take on all the aspects of turning your work into an e-book. You can always try one of these publishers as you yourself navigate your way around the new world of e-books.

Here are some e-book publishers to look up:

- Pugalicious Press (www.pugaliciouspress.com) is a small press based in New Hampshire, a small press that publishes stories for middle graders and young adults. They accept e-mail submissions of fantasy, high adventure, and historical fiction.
- Fictionwise (www.fictionwise.com) is a Barnes and Noble company. They publish fiction in all genres and non-fiction books too. Their website also has thousands of books to download in all different types of file format.
- Mushroom E-books (www.mushroom-ebooks.com) is part of Mushroom Publishing, a UK based print publisher. They publish fiction of all genres, particularly science fiction, fantasy, horror, thrillers and non-fiction such as travel writing, guide books, psychology, health, mind, body & spirit, biography and popular business books.
- Stonehedge Publishing (www.stonehedgepublishing.com) is an information packed website. Not only does it have submission guidelines, it also has articles and forums for prospective writers.
- E-book Crossroads (www.ebookcrossroads) has an A - Z directory of e-publishers for you to peruse if you want to find out more.

Just to note many e-book publishers get inundated with email submissions so they tend to have open times when they will accept manuscripts for their consideration and other times when submissions are not accepted. Check their websites for the most up-to-date information on submissions. If they are closed, call back at a later date.

E-book Rights

Any form of publishing rights can get complex and the laws concerning copyright, libel and territorial rights differ between countries. As an author you retain copyright on your work whether it is in print or electronic format. At a basic level, when you 'sell' a book to an e-book publisher, you are offering them the electronic or digital rights to your work. This means as well as publishing your e-book, they can use excerpts of your manuscript in other electronic formats, for instance, to be read on a mobile phone.

As the world of the e-book is still new to some publishers, there does seem to be grey areas around reproducing say a print book that is out of print and re-formatting it to an electronic version. I told you it was complex!

Read through any contract that you receive and make sure you understand what rights you are giving to an e-book publisher before you sign on the dotted line. The Society of Authors in the UK (www.societyofauthors.org) offers advice on contracts. Try The Writers Guild (www.wga.org) if you are based in the US and if you are in any doubt about your contract, make sure you get expert advice.

Chapter Nine

Promoting Yourself Online

What can you do to promote yourself as a writer and publicise your writing? If you are published, you may be invited to conferences or workshops to give a speech. If you are even luckier, you will be the main attraction at your own book signing. Even then people have to know that your event is on and they might want to know more about you before they attend. The Internet has opened up new ways of promoting yourself as a writer. It's not just about the work you do but your online personality too. Readers like to follow writers they are interested in to gain writing tips, to find out more about what makes a writer write and to perhaps see a more human side to the person they are following.

Using Social Media

Social media is really the way to go to keep in contact with your readers and other writers. In chapter seven, we looked at the top networking sites - Facebook, Twitter and LinkedIn. LinkedIn will connect you with other writers and professionals whilst Facebook and Twitter will link you to anyone around the globe who is interested in finding out more about you.

Many people don't feel comfortable about self-promotion but using these websites is not an in-your-face form of advertising. Social networks are more informal and chatty allowing you to post updates and talk to people interested in your work. I recently read somewhere that for every 10 posts, 8 should be of a personal nature and 2 should be promotional. In that case, readers really get to know you as a writer as well as what you actually write.

You don't have to bare your soul nor do you have to tell

everyone what you had for breakfast but it is interesting for other writers to find out more about what kind of person writes, where they find their ideas, whether they suffer from writer's block or what they enjoying writing about and what they don't.

There is another website that I hear writers are using and that is Pinterest (www.pinterest.com). It's a pin board kind of photo sharing site. Ok, you may have to take a look at it to see what I mean! You post photos of your interests, you can use other people's photos on your board or 'like' other people's photos. Here's where it works for writers - you can post pictures of your books, copies of magazines your articles or stories are in or use pictures of writing events and other things of interest that may appeal to fellow writers. If you prefer using visuals to writing lots of text then this site will be perfect for you.

Having your own Website

Some writers do and some writers don't. I'm one of those that doesn't at present. It's something that's on that never-ending to-do list of mine but I do use social media regularly and for now I'm happy enough having a Facebook page, LinkedIn and Twitter accounts. However I do manage a website for a writing college, The Writer's' Academy (www.thewritersacademy.net) so I have been through many permutations of website building and its up and downsides.

I started their website on a free site that allowed me to build a very basic but functional series of web pages. The problem was no-one ever saw it. It never came up on listings and it was never ranked in any search pages. So I changed provider, paid good money to have the site re-vamped and its ranking improved. Then the website host company put up their yearly fees so I changed company again but found out that the previous company had locked my IP address so there was a huge rigmarole about getting it unlocked. It's now with a company that has a small yearly fee for hosting but it's beginning to look dated and will need to go through the re-design process again soon.

Are you confused? I was. I thought you just got a website going and that was that. It stayed up in the cosmos and was available to anyone that looked for it through the Internet. I didn't know anything about SEO (search engine optimisation), the use of meta tags and hosting companies but I've gradually learnt to understand it all more and more. As I've said before, using the Internet is a learning process, and the more you use it, the more you feel comfortable and knowledgeable about its use. You don't ever have to get to the point where you could sit a Masters exam in computer technology but if you manage enough to keep your promotional wheels oiled then that's all you need to do.

I remember picking up a book when I was asked to design a website. I have computer qualifications so I thought this was going to be a doddle. The book was so confusing. I thought I'd never manage it but I did with the help of a free online website builder. There will always be websites that help you to build more websites online. It's just a matter of finding one that is right for you.

As a writer, if you want to have a website, you have two options, pay someone to do it for you or get stuck in to doing it yourself. Let's look at paying someone to do it for you first.

Getting Someone Else to Do it!

The main issue with going this route is the cost. Web design companies charge anything from a few hundred to a few thousand pounds. It depends exactly what you want your website to do. The more extra functions you want like having payment facilities or feedback forms, the more it costs. Yet you can find companies that will produce the basic package for you for a reasonable fee and if you really don't fancy designing your own site then this could be an option for you. Just remember that at some point you will want to update your information. You may have a new book out or you are speaking at a local event so you'll want that info to appear on your pages. If you have to pay a design company to write your updates then you will run into regular costs. It is possible to have a company set up your site but then you have a 'dashboard' so that at anytime you can go into your web pages and make the appropriate changes. Some dashboards are easier to use than others so make sure that you can work with their system.

When looking at a company to use, always, always look at the other websites they have produced. Check them to see whether you like their type of designs, whether the pages load quickly and whether they come up relatively early in a search. Ask to see a preview of your site before it goes live and do not be afraid of suggesting changes until you get the look you really want.

Find out what ongoing costs you will have to pay. Websites are hosted; that's how your website is connected to a web server, allowing it to be on the Internet and available for viewing at any given time. It doesn't have to be expensive but you will find that fees vary depending on which company or hosting service you use. The initial cost of buying a domain name - the name of your website - should be included in the package you choose but it will need to be renewed. This could be on a yearly basis or anytime up to ten years. Make sure you know what the costs of hosting, renewals and any other extras are and when you will be liable to pay them.

Doing It Yourself

I'm not going to suggest that you build a website from the ground up. It's tricky and if you really want to learn all about html, programming and website design then you might like to take a course or read the more technical books on the subject before you start.

There are many websites, however, that can start you off without you having to know all the ins and outs of running a website. Sites like Wix (www.wix.com) offer a free website building service where you can pick a template and add in your own information, photos and other images. Just browse the Internet for website builders and you will find a long list. Here are some of the best sites:

- Webs: www.webs.com
- Yola: www.yola.com
- Jigsy: www.jigsy.com
- Web Node: www.webnode.com
- Jimdo: www.jimdo.com
- Moonfruit: www.moonfruit.com
- Word Press: www.wordpress.org

Remember that having a website will promote you as a writer as well as your writing. In order for readers to regularly look at your web pages, you will need to update your information and include ways in which your followers can communicate with you. You can utilise feedback forms or invite people to email you. It's best to open a separate email account for your correspondence as a writer so that it doesn't interfere with your personal email account.

You will also have to think of ways to entice your followers to return to your site. There's no point in having a website up and running if no-one looks at it. You could have a tip for the week, offer free book giveaways or run a monthly competition. The time invested in connecting with your readers may well pay off in sales.

Promote your website or blog on all your social networks so that people can trace your work back to more information about you. If you write an article for another website, add all your social contact details. Link anything you do on the Net back to your website and this will help you to gain more visitors and hopefully, firm fans.

Blogging

Blogs are basically online diaries posted onto a blog or website at regular intervals whether that's a couple of times a week or once a month. Blogs are short entries of a few hundred words that don't take too long to read or write thus making them a great tool for promotion. They are also a great way of connecting you to a potential fan-base.

Blogs can be about anything but usually concentrate on one topic area and then have an angle within that. For instance, Catherine Ryan Howard used hers to let other writers know how she was getting on with being a self-published author. As well as letting people know more about the process she was going through, it also drew attention to her own book.

The idea then behind writing a blog is to regularly update your followers with first person, opinion type pieces of not more than around 500 words that allow readers to find out more about you as well as your work.

So what can your blog be about? Say for instance, you are commissioned to write a play or a TV script, you could use a blog to let other writers know how difficult or easy the task was. Perhaps you're researching a historical novel - that would make interesting reading, letting browsers know where you went and what you found out. Or you've started a writing group and can tell other writers how to go about it, who to contact for guest speakers and where other people can read your members' work.

To find out whether you are interested in using this form of connectivity, read other writers' blogs. Have a look at:

- Catherine, Caffeinated: www.catherineryanhoward.com
- Ask Allison: www.allisonwinnscotch.blogspot.ie
- Jeff Goins: www.goinswriter.com
- Terrible Minds: www.terribleminds.com/ramble/blog
- The Artist's Road: www.artistsroad.wordpress.com/

Some blogs have even built up to full length stories or have led to a novel being published. There is even The Blooker Prize - an award for books that come from blogs. So writing your own blog may draw attention from publishers as well as readers.

Setting up Your Own Blog

You'll be happy to know that there are websites that practically do it for you. Three of the easiest sites to use are Tumblr (www.tumblr.com), Posterous (www.posterous.com) and Overblog (www.over-blog.com). Tumblr aids new bloggers to start blogging within minutes. It's basic but functional and makes posting images or video clips an easy task. It boasts over 72 million blogs with over 70 million daily posts. Posterous is also a simplified blogging platform that makes it really easy to blog by allowing you to use your email account or mobile phone to post your writing. It also links to your social media accounts so there's really no excuse for not blogging!

I have a blog on Overblog but it came about in a rather strange way. I wrote for some months for Wikio Experts - a website content provider - that subsequently closed down. When it did several of my articles were posted onto a blog page. It was all done for me! The thing is I had no control over what blogs were posted so it is still a random mix of articles on everything from writing wedding invitations to ideas for arts and crafts sessions with the kids. It's on my to-do list to sort out!

For more experienced computer users, Google's Blogger (www.blogger.com) and Wordpress (www.wordpress.org) come highly recommended. Blogger lets you select a template that you then customise with background images, colours and fonts. Wordpress is similar but can be overly technical to newbie bloggers. However, if you are serious about using a blog to promote your work then Blogger and Wordpress give you more variety and control over your blog than the more simple platforms.

Having your Profile on other Websites

Promoting yourself online doesn't just mean having your own website and social networks. You can also promote yourself on other people's or organisations' websites. In Ireland, there is an Arts Council web site, that allows writers and other artists to post their profile on it. Sites like these could lead you to job opportunities or invites to writers' events. Check out your local arts council or department to see if they have a similar website. If you offer other writing services, you could list yourself on any local business websites for your area or if you teach any form of writing, make sure your details are on the relevant training and student pages for your locality or country.

Some other sites that promote writers and allow you to have your own profile posted on them are:

- Goodreads (www.goodreads.com) have an especially good author programme that is designed to help writers promote their books. It is designed mainly to allow authors with published books to promote their work but if you are self-published, you can add your work to their database. Other writers who are not yet published can still post excerpts of their writing for readers to comment on and review. When you create your profile with Goodreads, you can add book excerpts, publicise any events, share your favourite reads and even write a quiz about your book! They have a huge community of over 10,000,000 readers so it's well worth using them as a promotional tool.
- Library Thing (www.librarything.com) calls itself the world's largest book club. You can enter your details when you sign up as a member, import your own books, use their forums and get freebies to review.
- Red Room (www.redroom.com) encourages you to become a Red Room author and to post your books in their online bookstore. They also have excellent profile pages which

you can access if you take out their premium membership. This gives you a personal red room page where you can add your blog, your available books, your biography and published reviews. This is a really professional looking site that can help you to connect with more readers.

- Litopia Writer's Colony (www.litopia.com) is the Net's oldest community of writers. They help you to build an author's platform so that you can sell your work online. There is a subscription fee but you can try them out with a free 14 day trial.

- Filedby (www.filedby.com) is an online community used by many authors to promote their work. You can 'claim' a listing and have your own web presence and marketing platform. Filedby lists their authors' work on the Ingram database which is used by bookstores and libraries around the world linking you to much more than just their website. Every time you use this site, your updated information gets re-posted making it available to all the Filedby websites, thereby linking you with more potential customers.

The more profiles you have on various websites, the more you can attract new fans and followers to your writing. Get yourself out there so they can find you!

Online Advertising

This is probably more appropriate from a writer's point of view if you are trying to sell a book, especially if it is self-published or is in an e-book format. You can go to some lengths to create banner ads and pop-up advertisements if you are technically minded but the easiest way I have found of running an online advert is through Google's Adwords.

Adwords run those sponsored ads that come up when you use Google's search facility. So say you type in 'books for writers', the page will display its search results but also ads that have those keywords in them. Creating your advert with Adwords is easy. You choose your keywords so that you know what kind of searches your ad will appear alongside. You are only charged when a potential customer clicks on your ad - sorry, it's not free - but you can set a daily budget so that you never spend more on your advertising than you want to.

When your advert is clicked on, it goes through to your website or blog page where your book is ready for purchase. PayPal (www.paypal.com) is probably the easiest way of having a purchase function on your website although you may find others. It's easy to open a PayPal account from which you can access user 's tools and this allows you to generate a 'Buy Now' button that you can paste onto your site.

Using Email Newsletters

Another way of promoting yourself and your writing is to send out email newsletters. This can be done on a regular basis or just when you have something to promote. You can add a function on your website or blog that allows your readers to sign up for your newsletter or you can just begin compiling a list of email contacts that you send information to. However, if you are cold-calling your emails, it is wise to ask your contacts whether they wish to continue receiving email updates from you in the future. You don't want to put off potential readers by flooding their inbox with unwanted emails.

You can also use an auto responder to send emails out to your list of newsletter subscribers. Auto responders automatically send a reply email when someone contacts you but they can also be set to send out follow-up emails at regular intervals. Aweber (www.aweber.com) and Getresponse (www.getresponse.com) are two of the most popular auto responders. Look at their websites for further details of how they can manage your subscribers and email newsletters.

There are so many ways in which you can promote yourself and your writing using the Internet. Ok, so they can be time-consuming but just think of how many people you will reach across the globe. Build promotion into your weekly routine. You don't have to give it hours and hours especially if it begins to encroach on your writing time but putting aside an hour or two a week to promote yourself as a writer can only mean more connections, more opportunities and more sales. The Internet is there to be used and for the most part, its services are free. Make sure you get the most out of the Internet and promote yourself as a writer. There's a world of readers out there just waiting for your work!

Chapter Ten

Websites, Software and Resources for Writers

In this final chapter, I have listed websites that have appeared throughout this book and some new sites for you to look up. I've tried to include many of the things we have discussed that will help you, as a writer, to get the most out of the Internet. The following lists are by no means exhaustive and you will find many more on your travels through the web. Here are just some to get you started!

Useful Websites for Writers

Here is a selection of general websites for writers.

- Arts Council, England: www.artscouncil.org.uk
- Ask about Writing: www.askaboutwriting.net
- Author: www.author.co.uk
- Author-Network: www.author-network.com
- Copyright Licensing Agency: www.cla.co.uk
- E-Writers: www.e-writers.net
- Fiction Writers Connection: www.fictionwriters.com
- NaNoWriMo: www.nanowrimo.org
- National Endowment for the Arts (USA): www.arts.gov
- Plays On The Net: www.playsonthenet.com
- Poets and Writers: www.pw.org
- Reactive Writing: www.reactivewriting.co.uk
- Screenwriters Online: www.screenwriter.com
- The Irish Writers Centre: www.writerscentre.ie
- UK Children's Book Directory: www.ukchildrensbooks .co.uk
- Writers Net: www.writers.net

Organisations for Writers and Authors

Many writers' organisations have websites for you to keep up-to-date with the industry's latest news or find out more about joining an association that will benefit your writing life.

- Association of Authors and Publishers: www.authorsandpublishers.org
- Australian Society of Authors: www.asauthors.org
- Crime Writers Association: www.thecwa.co.uk
- Historical Writers Association: www.thehwa.co.uk
- Horror Writers Association: www.horror.org
- International Women's Writing Guild: www.iwwg.com
- National Union of Journalists: www.nuj.org.uk
- Science Fiction Writers of America: www.sfwa.org
- The Association of Authors Agents: www.agentassoc.co.uk
- The Authors Guild (USA): www.authorsguild.org
- The British fantasy Society: www.thebritishfantasysociety.co.uk
- The Society of Authors: www.societyofauthors.org
- The Society of Indexers: www.indexers.org.uk
- The Writers Guild of America: www.wga.org
- The Writers Guild of Canada: www.writersguildofcanada.com
- The Writers Guild Of Great Britain: www.writersguild.org.uk
- Writers Union of Canada: www.writersunion.ca

Web Directories

Help narrow your searches down by using an online web directory.

- Best of the Web Directory: www.botw.org
- Exact Seek: www.exactseek.com
- The Open Directory Project: www.dmoz.org

- Webotopia: www.webotopia.org

Article Directories

And for loads of online articles in every subject, check out:

- About: www.about.com
- Amazines: www.amazines.com
- Article Alley: www.articlealley.com
- Buzzle: www.buzzle.com
- Ezine Articles: www.ezinearticles.com
- Go Articles: www.goarticles.com
- Helium: www.helium.com

Reference Sites

When you need to do your research and look up extra facts, use some of these reference sites to increase your knowledge.

- About: www.about.com
- All Experts: www.allexperts.com
- Answers: www.answers.com
- Encyclopedia: www.encyclopedia.com
- How Stuff Works: www.howstuffworks.com
- Mahalo: www.mahalo.com
- Refdesk: www.refdesk.com
- Reference: www.reference.com
- Wikipedia: www.wikipedia.com

Genealogy Sites

Not only for checking out family history but also great for character research. Find out more about the past at:

- Ancestry: www.ancestry.co.uk
- Cyndi's List: www.cyndislist.com
- Find My Past: www.findmypast.com

- Genuki: www.genuki.org.uk
- Irish Genealogy: www.irishgenealogy.ie
- Olive Tree Genealogy: www.olivetreegenealogy.com/usa
- Roots Web: www.rootsweb.com
- The National Archives (UK): www.nationalarchives.gov.uk
- US National Archives: www.archives.gov

Archives

Delve deep into online archives to find out more information on any subject of your choice.

- Archive: www.archive.org
- Archives Hub: www.archiveshub.ac.uk
- Internet Classics Archive: www.classics.mit.edu
- The Internet Library of Early Journals: www.bodley.ox.ac.uk
- The National Academies Press: www.nap.edu

Writing Jobs

There are so many sites that advertise writing jobs but here are some that particularly target writers or offer online work themselves.

- About: www.about.com
- Craigs List: www.craigslist.com
- Constant Content: www.constant-content.com
- Demand Media studios: www.demandstudios.com
- Families: www.families.com
- Freelance Writing: www.freelancewriting.com
- Freelance Writing Gigs: www.freelancewritinggigs.com
- Hubpages: www.hubpages.com
- Online Writing Jobs: www.online-writing-jobs.com
- Skyword: www.skyword.com

- Squidoo: www.squidoo.com
- Textbroker: www.textbroker.com, www.textbroker.co.uk
- Wisegeek: www.wisegeek.com
- Words of Worth: www.wordsofworth.co.uk
- Writing World: www.writing-world.com

Free E-books

Who doesn't love a freebie? There are thousands of free e-books to download from these sites from classical works to those written by new authors.

- Bartleby: www.bartleby.com
- Bibliomania: www.bibliomania.com
- Book Yards: www.bookyards.com
- Free Books: www.freebooks.com
- Free E-books: www.free-ebooks.net
- Free Book Spot: www.freebookspot.es
- Globusz: www.globusz.com
- E-book Lobby: www.ebooklobby.com
- Online Free E-books: www.onlinefreeebooks.net
- Planet E-book: www.planetebook.com
- Project Gutenberg: www.gutenberg.org
- The E-books Directory: www.e-booksdirectory.com

Fiction and Poetry Websites

Sites where you can read fiction, post fiction, add a poem or get tips and advice as well as taking part in competitions.

- Backhand Stories: www.backhandstories.com
- Eastgate: www.eastgate.com
- Fan Story: www.fanstory.com
- Fiction on the Web: www.fictionontheweb.co.uk
- First Writer: www.firstwriter.com
- Fish Publications: www.fishpublishing.com

- Flash Fiction: www.flashfiction.net
- Flash Fiction Online: www.flashfictiononline.com
- Flash 500 Competition: www.flash500.com
- Ink Tears: www.inktears.com
- Playfic: www.playfic.com
- Protagonize: www.protagonize.com
- Poem: www.poem.org
- Poem Online: www.poetry.org
- Poem Hunter: www.poemhunter.com
- Poetry: www.poetry.com
- Storymash: www.storymash.com
- The Academy of American Poets: www.poets.org
- The Annual Interactive Fiction Competition: www.ifcomp.org
- The Dublin Review of Books: www.drb.ie
- The Internet Poets Co-operative: www.poetscoop.org
- The Never Ending Story: www.TheNeverEndingStory.com
- Wordstock Festival: www.wordstockfestival.com
- 101: One Zero One: www.iceflow.com/onezeroone/101/OneZeroOne.html.

Humourous Websites

Have a laugh and look out for writing possibilities at the same time with some of these funny websites.

- Break: www.break.com
- Cracked: www.cracked.com
- College Humor: www.collegehumor.com
- Comedy Central: www.comedycentral.com/
- Ebaums World: http://www.ebaumsworld.com/
- Funny or Die: www.funnyordie.com
- News Biscuit: www.newsbiscuit.com

Writing Courses

If you're looking for some expert help and guidance, you could take a course and learn some new skills from one of these course providers.

- Chrysalis - The Poet in You: www.lotusfoundation.org.uk
- Creuse Writers Workshop and Retreat: www.creusewritersworkshopandretreat.com
- Fire in the Head: www.fire-in-the-head.co.uk
- Literature Training: www.literaturetraining.com
- London School of Journalism: www.lsj.org
- National Council for the Training of Journalists, UK: www.nctj.com
- Open College of the Arts: www.oca-uk.com
- The Arvon Foundation: www.arvonfoundation.org
- The Big Smoke Writing Factory: www.bigsmokewritingfactory.com
- The Publishing Training Centre: www.train4publishing.co.uk
- The Writers Academy: www.thewritersacademy.net
- The Writers Bureau: www.writersbureau.com
- Writers News Home Study Courses: www.writersonline.co.uk/home-study

Writing Tools and Software

Everyone needs a little help at times - check out these writers' tools to see if they can give you a helping hand.

- Celtx: www.celtx.com
- Characterisation Tool: www.synergise.com/p4
- Evernote: www.evernote.com
- Plagiarism Checker: www.copyscape.com
- Scrivener: www.literatureandlatte.com
- Story Wizard: www.storywizard.co.uk

- The New Novelist: www.newnovelist.com
- Write or Die: www.writeordie.com
- Word Counter: www.wordcounter.com
- Wunderlist: www.6wunderkinder.com/wunderlist

Cloud Services

Relatively new on the computer scene, cloud services need a little explanation. A cloud service provider offers people a way to store their data through a private or public network via the Internet. This means you can share files from one of the below services without them clogging up your computer.

- Dropbox: www.dropbox.com
- Google Docs: www.google.com/docs
- Sky Drive: www.explore.live.com/skydrive

E-book Publishers

Want to write an e-book or have a manuscript ready to send out? Check out some of these publishers to see if your work fits their lists.

- Avid Press: www.avidpress.com
- Artemis Press: www.artemispress.com
- Atlantic Bridge: www.atlanticbridge.net
- Crowsnest: www.computercrowsnest.com
- Diskus Publishing: www.diskuspublishing.com
- Enovel: www.enovel.com
- Fiction Works: www.fictionworks.com
- John Hunt Publishing: www.johnhuntpublishing.com
- Loveyoudivine Alterotica: www.loveyoudivine.com
- Online Originals: www.onlineoriginals.com
- Treeless Press: www.treeless.com
- Word Wrangler: www.wordwrangler.com

E-book Software

Download e-book software so that you can read e-books and produce your own.

- Calibre: www.calibre-ebook.com
- Mobipocket: www.mobipocket.com
- Scribus: www.scribus.net
- Smashwords: www.smashwords.com

PDF Converters

Whether you have Word files to convert to PDF or have other file types that you want to convert, some of these websites will be able to help.

- Convert Word to PDF: www.doc2pdf.net
- Free PDF Converter: www.freepdfconvert.com
- PDF Online: www.pdfonline.com
- Primo PDF: www.primopdf.com
- Word to PDF: www.wordtopdf.com

Photo Images Sites

Looking for cover pictures? Need to pick out photos or images? Choose from thousands of royalty free images on the following sites.

- Dreamstime: www.dreamstime.com
- Flickr: www.flickr.com
- Free Digital Photos: www.freedigitalphotos.net
- Istock: www.istockphoto.com
- Jupiter Images: www.jupiterimages.com
- Morguefile: www.morguefile.com
- Shutterstock: www.shutterstock.com
- Stock Free Images: www.stockfreeimages.com

Design Software

If you want to design book covers that will really impress your readers and stand out from the crowd, look up these design software sites.

- Adobe Indesign: www.adobe.com/products/indesign
- Gimp:www.gimp.org
- Photoshop: www.adobe.com
- Picasa: www.picasa.google.co.uk
- Pixelmator: www.pixelmator.com
- Quark Xpress: www.quark.com/Products/QuarkXPress

Online Resources for Writers' Block

Ok so everyone gets stumped at times. Release your writers' block by trying out some online writing prompts.

- Creative Writing Prompts: www.creativewritingprompts .com
- Creativity Portal: www.creativity-portal.com/prompts /imagination.prompt.html
- Plinky: www.plinky.com
- The Story Starter: www.thestorystarter.com
- The Writers Block Online: www.thewritingblockonline .com
- Toasted Cheese: www.toasted-cheese.com
- Writing Fix: www.writingfix.com/classroom_tools/daily promptgenerator.html

Dictionary and Thesauri Sites

Not just for looking up correct spellings or alternative word use, these sites often have extras to increase your knowledge as a wordsmith.

- Collins Dictionary: www.collinsdictionary.com

- Dictionary of Slang: www.dictionaryofslang.co.uk
- Dictionary Reference: www.dictionary.reference.com
- Merriam Webster: www.merriam-webster.com
- Oxford Dictionaries: www.oxforddictionairies.com
- Roget's Thesaurus: www.education.yahoo.com
- Thesaurus: www.thesaurus.com
- Your Dictionary: www.yourdictionary.com

Website Builders

Get started on building your own website with templates, help and support from these sites.

- Jigsy: www.jigsy.com
- Jimdo: www.jimdo.com
- Moonfruit: www.moonfruit.com
- Web Node: www.webnode.com
- Webs: www.webs.com
- Word Press: www.wordpress.org
- Yola: www.yola.com

Blogs

Read some of the most entertaining blogs from fellow writers before you start your own.

- Ask Allison: www.allisonwinnscotch.blogspot.ie
- Catherine, Caffeinated: www.catherineryanhoward.com
- Jeff Goins: www.goinswriter.com
- Terrible Minds: www.terribleminds.com/ramble/blog
- The Artist's Road: www.artistsroad.wordpress.com/

Setting Up your Own Blog

Start your own blog with help from one of these sites.

- Google's Blogger: www.blogger.com

- Overblog: www.over-blog.com
- Posterous: www.posterous.com
- Tumblr: www.tumblr.com
- Wordpress: www.wordpress.org

Profile Websites

Promote yourself online by adding your profile to one of these sites.

- Filedby: www.filedby.com
- Goodreads: www.goodreads.com
- Library Thing: www.librarything.com
- Litopia Writer's Colony: www.litopia.com
- Red Room: www.redroom.com
- Scribd: www.scribd.com

Grammar

Practice your grammar or find the answers to those tricky grammar questions.

- Daily Grammar: www.dailygrammar.com
- Grammar Book: www.grammarbook.com
- Grammarly: www.grammarly.com
- Guide to Grammar and Style: www.andromeda.rutgers.edu/~jlynch/Writing

Writing Guidelines

Check out individual publishers and magazines for their guidelines or look up more general advice on the following sites.

- The Author Network: www.author-network.com
- The Eclectic Writer: www.eclectics.com
- Writer's Digest: www.writersdigest.com
- Writers Guidelines Database: www.writerswrite.com

Writers' Forums

Chat to other writers, ask for advice and share your own experiences on one of these writers' forums.

- Absolute Write: www.absolutewrite.com
- NaNoWriMo: www.nanowrimo.org
- The Writer's Digest Forum: www.writersdigest.com
- The Writing Room: www.writingroom.com
- Writers: www.writers.net
- Writers Cafe: www.writerscafe.org
- Writers Weekly: www.writersweekly.com

Critique Sites

Need some advice on your work? Post your writing on a critique site for comments and feedback from other writers.

- Authonomy: www.authonomy.com
- Critique Circle: www.critiquecircle.com
- Ladies Who Critique: www.ladieswhocritique.com
- My Writers Circle: www.mywriterscircle.com
- Review Fuse: www.reviewfuse.com
- Scribophile: www.scribophile.com
- The Desk Drawer: www.winebird.com
- Writing : www.writing.com

The Fun Stuff!

Time to play! Everyone needs a break at times; use yours creatively with a word game from one of these sites.

- East of the Web: www.eastoftheweb.com
- Fun with Words: www.fun-with-words.com
- Gamehouse: www.gamehouse.com
- Games: www.games.com
- Shockwave: www.shockwave.com

- Word Games: www.wordgames.com
- Word Games: www.wordgames.net
- Wordplays: www.wordplays.com

Contacting the Author

I would love to know how this book has helped you, what websites have worked well for you and how you are getting the most out of using the Internet as a writer. You can find me on Facebook, Twitter and LinkedIn if you want to make contact.

- Facebook: www.facebook.com/SarahBWatkinsWriter
- Twitter: @SarahBWatkins
- LinkedIn: Sarah-Beth Watkins

You can also look up more about Compass Books and John Hunt Publishing on

- Compass Books: www.compass-books.net
- Facebook: www.facebook.com/JHPCompassBooks
- John Hunt Publishing: www.johnhuntpublishing.com

Please note that whilst every effort has been made to ensure that these websites are up and running, websites die off or are replaced with new sites every day. Happy searching!

**COMPASS
BOOKS**

Compass Books focuses on practical and informative 'how-to' books for writers. Written by experienced authors who also have extensive experience of tutoring at the most popular creative writing workshops, the books offer an insight into the more specialised niches of the publishing game.